teach yourself
paper crafts
projects | tips | techniques

Paper crafting and the preservation of memorabilia is one of the fastest growing hobbies today. Whether you want to make your own journals, greeting cards, and invitations, or create scrapbooks of family photos to document special occasions, a whole new genre of products and creative ideas is waiting for you.

As you look through these pages, you'll be introduced to tools and techniques used to make paper crafts, and you'll find simple instructions and patterns for completing a myriad of projects. It's never been easier—with a little knowledge, some imagination, and a minimal investment of time and money, you can enjoy many satisfying hours of creativity.

Enjoy.

Page 28

Page 82

Page 74

Contents

Page 45

Page 49

paper crafts **basics**

Paper Crafts
basics

Once you know the basics, you'll enjoy creating the projects featured in this book—and you'll be ready to design originals of your own. The materials you use are very important. How you use them is up to you.

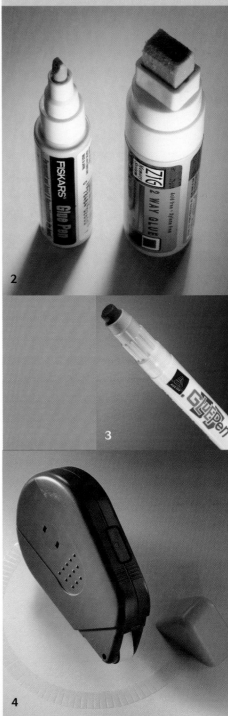

Tools and Materials

Adhesives Acid-free and photo-safe adhesives for paper crafts and scrapbooking come in an amazing variety of products, including repositionable types. The choice you make depends on the desired results.

Glue Pens, Glue Sticks, and Markers—1, 2, and 3
Designed with tips in assorted sizes and shapes, some of these products dispense glue in a line as fine as that made by a ballpoint pen. Larger tips such as glue sticks *(1)* are flat and can quickly cover large areas, or use chiseled tips *(2)* and glue pens *(3)* for more precise placement of adhesive. Some glues roll on white or a light color, then turn clear when dry. Tinted glues are easier to see as the glue is being applied. Different adhesives can be used for either a permanent or repositionable bond.

Liquid Glues *(not shown)*
Some are as thin as water; others are thick. The best adhesives for gluing large areas are those that don't cause wrinkles. Always experiment with the product before starting the project and plan your design so that you can place elements accurately the first time.

Spray Adhesives *(not shown)*
Available in aerosol cans, these adhesives are often repositionable and provide an even, overall layer of glue with a touch of the nozzle. Spray glues cover large surfaces

quickly with minimal mess and work well for adhering background papers and photo mats.

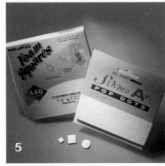

Tapes, Mounting Adhesives, and Double-Sided Foam Adhesive—4 and 5
Available with or without a dispenser, most double-sided tapes come in rolls of narrow, clear tape protected with peel-away paper. The tape is cut to the desired length and applied to the project, then the release paper is removed. Some handheld refillable dispenser styles *(4)* roll a band of thin tape directly onto the paper craft surface. Mounting adhesives are double-sided precut pieces measuring up to ½" square. Most are packaged on a roll in a self-dispensing box, but some are available in handheld dispensers with roller-wheel tips for applying the squares one at a time. Double-sided foam-adhesive dots and squares *(5)* add dimension and design interest to paper crafts. About ⅛" thick and no larger than ½" wide, the double-sided foam-adhesive shapes are protected with peel-away paper. Use them behind die cuts, letters, and cropped photos.

1

Creasing Tool—1

Made of plastic or bone, this tool—also called a bone folder—is used for scoring and making sharp, clean creases on paper. The pointed end is for scoring and the rounded end for creasing.

Crimping Tool *(not shown)*

This device turns flat paper into corrugated paper and adds dimension and texture to projects.

Cutting Mat, Self-Healing—2

Cutting mats are available in a variety of sizes and help protect surfaces when using rotary cutters, crafts knives, and other cutting tools. The lines and rulers help align materials when cutting.

Embellishments

Use embellishments to personalize and enhance paper crafts by highlighting photos, adding dimension, or creating a theme. Although many items can be used as embellishments, the following are most often used:

Die Cuts—3

Die cuts, premade paper shapes available at most scrapbook and crafts stores, come in many shapes, sizes, and colors. For a fee, some stores will let you use their die-cutting machine and your own papers to create shapes that coordinate with your layouts.

Stickers—4

Acid-free, photo-safe stickers come in thousands of different themes and sizes and are widely available in sheets and rolls.

Punches—5

Available in a variety of shapes and sizes, decorative paper punches let you create custom accents in shapes from any papers that complement your layout.

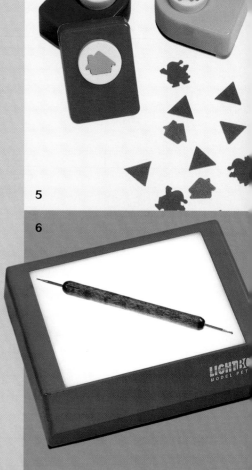

5

6

Light Box—6

Used as a light source behind paper, a light box allows you to make embossed paper. **Note:** *See light box on* page 12.

Metal Ruler *(not shown)*

This type of ruler has a thin layer of cork on the bottom. Use it as a guide for cutting paper with a crafts knife or makin straight lines with pens and markers. This is the ruler of choice for many paper crafters as ink will not run under the edge, causing smears and blurred lines.

Page Sleeves *(not shown)*

Also referred to as plastic page protectors, page sleeves slip over finished album pages to help protect the entire page from dust an fingerprints; they also prevent photos on facing pages from rubbing together. Sleeves are available in side-loading or top-loading styles in 8½×11" or 12×12" page sizes. Prote individual photos by slipping them into clear plastic photo sleeves that attach to the page with an adhesive backing. Page sleeve allow photos to be changed later if desired.

2

3

4

Paper and Card Stock–7

Ensure the longevity of your paper crafts by using only materials that are acid-free and lignin-free, or labeled "of archival quality" or "photo safe." Products that are acid-free and lignin-free have a pH factor of 7.0 or above, and do not yellow or damage your photographs.

If acidic paper is used, such as a newspaper clipping, the acid will transfer to the acid-free paper, turning it yellow or brown. Use a de-acidification spray or make a photocopy of the item using acid-free copy paper. An acid-testing pen also is available where scrapbook and paper craft supplies are sold) to help you check papers that aren't labeled.

Acid-free paper and card stock are available at scrapbook, hobby, and art stores. Standard-size papers include 4×6", 5×7", 8½×11", and 12×12" pages in a multitude of colors, designs, and finishes. Available in solid colors, card stock is the weight most paper crafters prefer for backgrounds, greeting cards, punched embellishments, and die cuts. Patterned papers typically are lighter weight and are offered in thousands of colors, textures, and designs. Commonly available specialty papers include vellum, embossed card stock, handmade paper, and paper with metallic finishes.

Pens, Pencils, and Markers

Many writing utensils are safe to use on paper crafts, but look for those labeled "acid-free" or "photo-safe." Also choose products that will resist bleeding and fading. All come in a plethora of colors and sizes.

Colored Pencils–8

Available in hundreds of hues, colored pencils are a paper crafters' staple, ideal for shading, adding highlights to lettering, and creating embellishments. Use them with a blender—a clear, colorless pencil or pen—to smooth and soften the colors.

Felt-tip Markers

Markers are used in many ways—for letters, borders, illustrations, captions, and color on rubber stamps. They are available in a variety of nibs, colors, and sizes for creating endless techniques. There are four basic types:

Brush Tip–**9** The nib on a brush-point marker is as flexible as a paintbrush. Similar to a paintbrush, the thinness of the line depends upon the pressure exerted. Write with the brush on its side—not on the tip, using zigzag strokes. Use heavier pressure for a wide downstroke and lighter pressure going up. Brush markers also are handy for coloring rubber stamps or making colorful drawings.

Chisel Point–**10** This versatile marker is capable of producing a variety of decorative styles. Beginners should first experiment by turning the tip different ways to learn to make both broad and narrow strokes. Master the use of this marker by taking a class in calligraphy.

Monoline–**11** Monoline markers have round, tapered nibs and create continuous lines with no variation in thickness. Nib sizes range from very fine (.005) to thick and are considered to be all-purpose markers for basic lettering techniques, captions, borders, illustrations, and line art.

Scroll Tip–**12** Scroll-tip markers are similar to chisel-tip markers, except the center of the tip is notched to create a double line. Use it to vary lettering styles and achieve unique looks.

Gel Pens *(not shown)*

These medium-line pens are ideal for journaling, outlining letters, and embellishing paper crafts.

Photo Corners *(not shown)*

Photo corners are triangular with peel-away backings; they are used to attach photos directly to a layout.

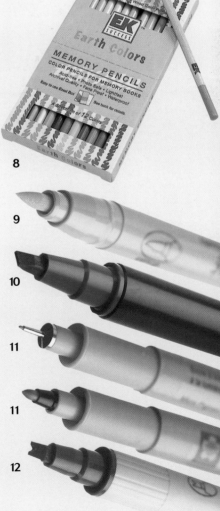

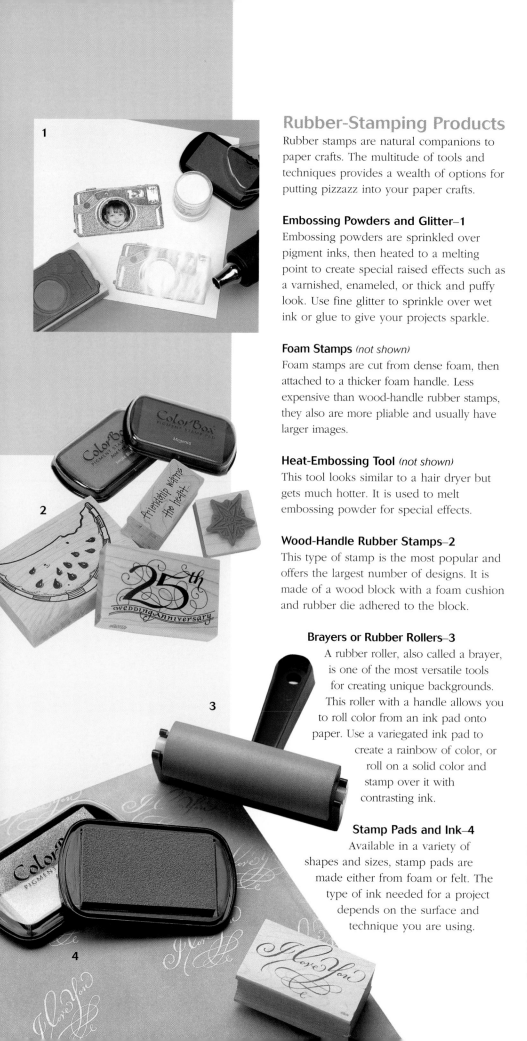

Rubber-Stamping Products

Rubber stamps are natural companions to paper crafts. The multitude of tools and techniques provides a wealth of options for putting pizzazz into your paper crafts.

Embossing Powders and Glitter–1

Embossing powders are sprinkled over pigment inks, then heated to a melting point to create special raised effects such as a varnished, enameled, or thick and puffy look. Use fine glitter to sprinkle over wet ink or glue to give your projects sparkle.

Foam Stamps *(not shown)*

Foam stamps are cut from dense foam, then attached to a thicker foam handle. Less expensive than wood-handle rubber stamps, they also are more pliable and usually have larger images.

Heat-Embossing Tool *(not shown)*

This tool looks similar to a hair dryer but gets much hotter. It is used to melt embossing powder for special effects.

Wood-Handle Rubber Stamps–2

This type of stamp is the most popular and offers the largest number of designs. It is made of a wood block with a foam cushion and rubber die adhered to the block.

Brayers or Rubber Rollers–3

A rubber roller, also called a brayer, is one of the most versatile tools for creating unique backgrounds. This roller with a handle allows you to roll color from an ink pad onto paper. Use a variegated ink pad to create a rainbow of color, or roll on a solid color and stamp over it with contrasting ink.

Stamp Pads and Ink–4

Available in a variety of shapes and sizes, stamp pads are made either from foam or felt. The type of ink needed for a project depends on the surface and technique you are using.

Crafters or Fabric Ink: This multipurpose ink is designed for use on wood, metal, paper, and fabrics. It is available in solvent and water-base formulas. Always heat-set the ink when using on fabric.

Dye-Based Ink: Available in many colors, these water-base inks are quick drying. However, they may bleed or blur when used on absorbent papers such as construction and tissue paper.

Pigment Ink: Available in a multitude of colors and metallics, pigment inks are thick, opaque, and slow drying. They work well on all types of papers but will not dry on glossy-coated paper unless an embossing technique is used.

Scissors and Cutting Tools

A variety of scissors and cutting tools are necessary for paper crafting. Some are for getting the job done; others are for embellishing.

Circle and Oval Cutters *(not shown)*

These adjustable tools make circles and ovals of various sizes to crop photos, create mats, and embellish paper projects. Use a self-healing or glass cutting mat when working with these sharp instruments.

Crafts and Swivel Knives *(not shown)*

Crafts knives are perfect for making straight cuts on paper, card stock, and photos. Swivel knives are similar to crafts knives but they have a rotating blade that makes them better for cutting around curves, letters, and template shapes. Use these sharp tools with a self-healing or glass cutting mat.

Decorative-Edge Scissors–5 *(shown opposite)*

Decorative-edge scissors are ideal for cutting photo mats and for giving lacy edges to cards or any project you want to have a dressier look.

Paper Trimmer *(shown on page 9)*

Paper trimmers are a must for making perfect square cuts and straight edges. The larger sizes are capable of handling even oversize sheets of paper and card stock.

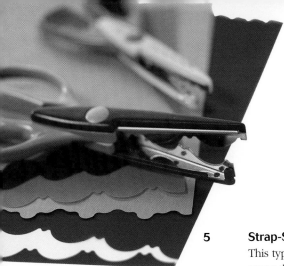

5

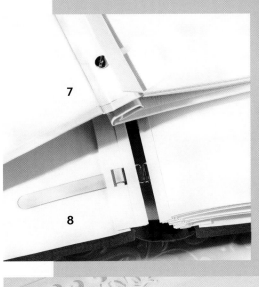

7

8

Strap-Style–8

This type of album is held together with straps that allow the pages to lie completely flat when open.

Rotary Cutters *(not shown)*
Often used to cut fabric, rotary cutters also are handy for cutting large sheets of paper, card stock, or photos. Use these tools with self-healing or glass cutting mats.

Straight-Edge Scissors *(not shown)*
Long straight-edge scissors are useful for cutting large sheets of card stock and paper or for freehand cropping photos. Small scissors work best for cutting out detailed embellishments.

Scrapbook Albums

Scrapbook albums are available in standard sizes of 5×7", 8½×11", and 12×12". Check to see whether the album is designed to accommodate page protectors if you intend to use them. The most popular album types are the following:

Spiral-Bound–6
Albums with spiral wire binding have permanently attached pages and are ideal for one-topic and themed scrapbooks.

Post-Bound–7
Post-bound albums are well-suited for adding or rearranging pages. The albums use a set of threaded bolts to bind the pages together.

Three-Ring *(not shown)*
The most common type of album, these familiar favorites have rings that snap apart for easy page insertion and removal.

Stylus—*(shown on page 4)*
Use a stylus to make embossed designs on paper. This pen-shape tool has a ballpoint tip on each end. The large end is used for less intricate areas; the small end creates, more precise details.

Templates and Stencils–9
Embossing stencils are available in either brass or plastic; brass stencils produce the sharpest embossed images due to the thickness and the crispness of the cutout. Take advantage of the many shapes and sizes of plastic templates and stencils to crop photos, make lettering, and create embellishments.

Xyron Machine–10
Capable of turning paper items into ready-to-adhere stickers, the Xyron machine is mess-free. With a twist of the knob, adhesive is applied to the back of the item and the item is backed with removable paper.

9

Create your own stencil using blank stencil plastic and a hand punch, as shown above.

10

6

Techniques

Collecting Meaningful Items

Save small items such as menus, place mats, brochures, and business cards that relate to your paper craft themes. Remember also to save newspaper clippings, magazine articles, programs, brochures, announcements, matchbooks, and tickets. Even objects from nature such as seashells, dried flowers, or leaves make interesting mementos and add interest to your projects.

Creasing Paper
(opposite bottom and above right)

As your newest card or paper projects unfold, focus on the folds. Before you work with your next piece of paper, learn the correct way to score and fold it.

Finding the Grain: When folding paper, it's important to first find the paper grain—the direction in which paper fibers align. Paper folded parallel to the grain produces cleaner and stronger folds and lies flatter, which is important in paper crafting.

To find the grain of the paper, gently curl a sheet of paper across the length of the paper. Let it uncurl, and then curl it across the width. The direction that offers the least resistance is with the grain.

Scoring: Although thin papers don't require scoring, heavyweight papers must be scored before they are folded. Use the pointed end of a creasing tool (also called a bone folder) for scoring and the rounded end for creasing. Other tools that can be used for scoring are a dull butter knife, a dry ballpoint pen, or an embossing stylus.

To score a sheet of paper, first mark it lightly with a very sharp pencil along the top and bottom edges. Align a ruler along the pencil marks, and with the pointed end of the creasing tool or other folding tool, run it along the edge of the ruler hard enough to make a line or groove in the paper.

Creasing: To crease the paper, fold down one edge of the paper, matching corners. Place the creasing tool (*above*) or other tool along the center of the fold. Press lightly with the side of the tool, moving it from the center to one edge, then to the opposite edge. Sometimes creasing with a creasing tool causes shine along the crease. Prevent the shine by placing a scrap of paper on the fold and then running the creasing tool along both papers.

Cropping *(center opposite)*

Cropping, or trimming, a photo involves a variety of techniques and tools and can improve its composition. Photos with dark or light areas and busy or undesirable backgrounds should be cropped. Keep the following guidelines in mind:

• Be careful not to cut away important bits of history. An old family car, portions of clothing, or a piece of furniture in the background may seem unnecessary details today, but could prove sentimentally invaluable in the years to come.

• Make several prints or photocopies of the same image for practice. When you are pleased with the results, crop the actual photo you will be using and glue it in the layout.

Use a creasing tool (bone folder) to make a neat crease and fold in the paper.

A rotary paper trimmer works for repetitive scoring and cutting of paper, and the rolling blade is interchangeable with decorative blades.

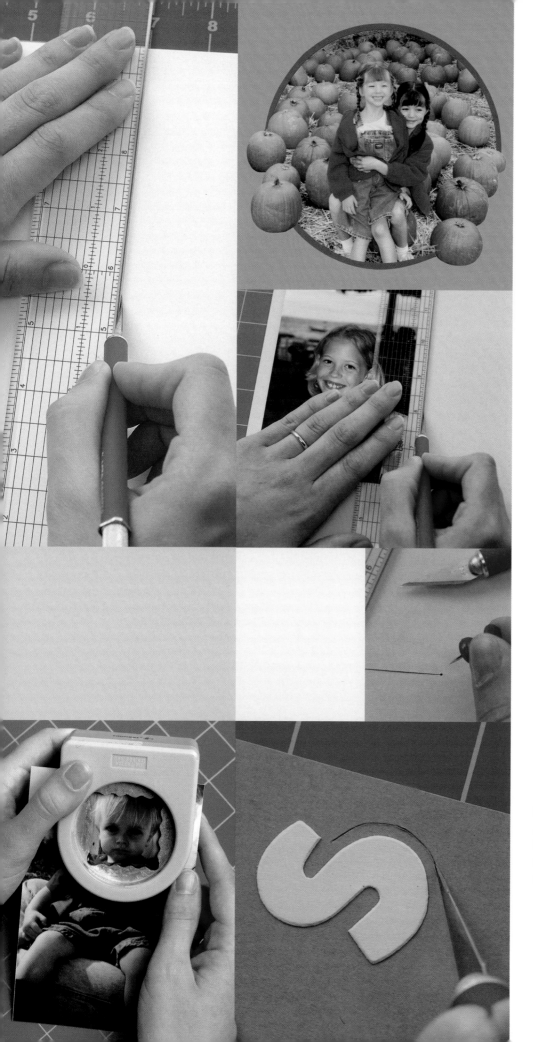

- Polaroid photos should not be cropped because the chemicals used to develop the photo can leak when cut and damage your paper craft projects.
- Use a sharp crafts knife and ruler to trim photos, *center left*. A small pair of scissors is best for cutting out silhouettes or trimming away backgrounds.
- Creatively display a photo inside a shape. Use circle cutters or transparent templates to create a variety of shapes such as circles, ovals, numerals, stars, flowers, and even birthday cakes.
- To cut rectangular or square shapes, use a quality ruler, a 90-degree triangle, or a cropping square and a crafts knife.
- Use punches to cut out small images such as a face or small animal, *below left*.
- Cut frames or mats from patterned paper and place over a photo to create a cropped effect.
- Make a silhouette by cutting out a shape around a figure as shown in the girls in the pumpkin patch example *above right*. For a photo that has already been silhouetted, mount it on a thin mat of colored card stock. To add interest to a shape, try silhouetting part of the image. Put children into a newspaper cartoon, sitting on top of a skyscraper, riding a dinosaur, or lifting a building.
- Look for templates that you may already have in your home. Jar lids make great circles, and cookie cutters are perfect for shapes, especially for the holidays.
- Keep your cropping simple so it doesn't detract from the subject of the photo.

Cutting and Trimming

A crafts knife can be a paper crafter's best friend—or enemy. Torn paper, accidental cuts, and nicked fingers are some challenges of cutting shapes.

- Nothing improves your cutting better than a sharp blade. Replace your blades often. If you do a lot of cutting, consider purchasing the more expensive stainless-steel blades that stay sharp longer.

- For better control when cutting a straight edge, cut the paper by pulling the knife toward you. Avoid cutting anything horizontally.
- Protect the area that you plan to save. If one side of what you cut is going to be a scrap, make sure the ruler covers the good side. If the knife slips, you'll cut into the scrap, not into the finished piece.
- Be aware of the angle of the blade. Try to keep it perpendicular to the ruler.
- Use a pushpin to mark the end of where you plan to cut. When the knife comes to the hole, the knife will naturally stop at the correct place without overshooting it, *opposite center*.
- When cutting several layers of paper at once, start with two sheets of paper, then three, then four—working your way up to the greatest number that is successful. Don't get too ambitious; at some point, your cuts will become inaccurate.
- To make a neat cut in thick paper, make two passes with the knife—apply even pressure and you'll have more control. For extrathick items, such as foam core or mat board, lubricate the blade with Thread Ease or Sewer's Aid. These products are used to lubricate sewing thread and also work well on knife blades. Always test the blade on scrap material before cutting.
- When cutting a shape with inside angles, position the paper so you always start the cut on the inside and pull the knife to the outside of the shape, as shown *opposite, below right*.
- To save time when making a long, straight cut without a straightedge, hold the knife like a pencil so that the end of the handle is in your palm and your index finger rests on the top (the dull edge) of the blade. This technique will cause the knife to travel in a nearly perfect straight line.

Embossing
Heat Embossing
Embossing over a rubber-stamped image gives it a raised appearance that adds dimension to the page. Try cutting out the embossed images and using them as elements on your paper crafts.

Getting started: Using pigment ink, stamp the image onto your paper. While the ink is still wet, sprinkle embossing powder over the entire stamped image. Tap the excess powder off the image and return it to the original container. Moving a heat-embossing tool back and forth, *above right*, hold it one to two inches from the image until the powder begins to melt. The image will take on a glossy, raised appearance as the powder melts.

Different types of embossing powders produce different effects. Clear embossing powders create a shiny finish with a look similar to varnish or enamel when stamped over colored inks. Extreme embossing powders produce a thick puffy appearance.

Suede Paper Embossing

Try embossing on suede paper, *center right*, using a rubber stamp to create the design. The texture of the suede paper allows the imprint of a stamp to be applied using heat from an iron. Choose a stamp with chunky detail rather than fine detail, which won't show up.

To emboss the paper, lay the paper face down on top of the rubber stamp. Using an iron set on medium heat, press the iron on top of the paper. Pull the paper off the stamp to reveal the imprint. Try cutting out embossed designs and using them as elements on your paper crafts, or emboss a whole piece of paper and use it as a background.

Pressure (Dry) Embossing
The raised look of pressure-embossed images, *below right*, such as raised lettering, fancy edges, or graphic elements can add subtle texture and dramatic effects to your paper crafts. Virtually any paper project can benefit from the unique addition of embossing.

You will need a light source behind the paper, such as a light box or a window. To

Brass or plastic stencils are essential for creating pressure-embossed images.

Step 1 Using a light box, a sunny window, or a glass table with a lamp placed underneath it, place the template upside down on the light source and tape the edges with masking tape.

Step 2 Place paper or vellum over the template, tape it in place, and apply pressure with the tip of the stylus inside the edges of the stencil to press the design into the paper.

Step 3 Shown *above* is the raised image after embossing.

position the embossed image accurately (see *Step 1*). Light-colored papers are easier to emboss because they allow more light to pass through than darker papers. When using dark-colored paper, feel the paper to locate and adjust the position of the stencil underneath the paper.

Using a stylus, apply pressure and draw it along the inner cut edges of the stencil to create indentations in the paper (see *Step 2*). Use the small ballpoint end for embossing small detailed areas and the larger end for less intricate areas. See *Step 3* for the final results.

Journaling

Journaling is usually handwritten and allows readers not only to read about memorable events of the past, family celebrations, and special activities but also to get insight into your personality. Recollections that may seem trivial at the time, such as weather, what you ate, a travel situation, or something funny that happened, may prove fascinating to those who read your scrapbook pages years from now. As you plan journaling for a scrapbook page, keep these tips in mind:

• When journaling, the writing should connect the page viewer with the actual event. Record more than just titles, dates, and names. Describe your reactions to what was happening, tell what the subject was doing and why, and share your feelings about the event.

• Have someone proofread a draft of your journaling before you add it to the page. Check also for spelling and grammatical errors.

• Perfect your penmanship. Try writing your text in pencil before going over it in pen.

• Create interest by journaling in shapes such as circles, hearts, and wavy or diagonal lines for variety.

• Find the right pen and paper combination. Some people enjoy working with ballpoint pens on newsprint. Gel pens are very popular and have a nice feel on all-purpose paper.

• Place your journaling paper on a cushion of several sheets of paper. It makes it much easier to write.

• Good handwriting doesn't happen by accident. Slow down and spend some time working on using rhythmic strokes and shapes.

Matting

Make your photos, journaling, and memorabilia stand out on the page with mats. Coordinate matting colors and textures with your photographs and memorabilia so they'll enhance rather than detract from the subjects.

To create a simple photo mat, use a background paper or card stock that's slightly larger than your photo. Position the photo on the mat, and adhere it with archival-quality adhesive. Then trim the mat with straight or decorative-edge scissors, a crafts knife, or a paper trimmer.

Common Errors in Journaling

Mixing printed and cursive letters

printing and cursive

Small letters begin to close up

small and tight

Inconsistent spacing gives your lettering a sloppy look

inconsistent spacing

Rounded letters have dissimilar shapes

round letters

Inconsistent slant gives your lettering a sloppy look

inconsistent slant

Photographing for Your Projects

Photos will be the focal points of many of your projects. Here are some tips to get the best possible shots.

• The best photos are unposed and capture the personality of the subjects. Keep a small notebook with you so you can write down names, places, dates, and other pertinent information about the people and places you photograph.

• Try to position the camera no more than 8 feet from the subject.

• Take one shot of the people, and then take a second shot of the background in order to set the mood.

• Have your subject face the sun, or keep the sun behind your own shoulder. Early morning and late afternoon on a sunny day are the ideal times for taking pictures.

• Make sure the lighting is correct when taking photos indoors or at night. To prevent your photos from looking flat, consider using a light source placed in the right location to create shadows and dimension (see Halloween photos, *top right*).

• Rather than place your subject directly in the center of the photo, adjust your frame so the subject is about one-third of the way from the edge.

• Glue the original photos to your project, or make color photocopies and save the originals for other purposes. Choosing the right photocopier to reproduce quality photos for projects is key. Shown at *right*, from *top to bottom:* The clean original photo; a good black-and-white copy from a color copier that shows detail; and a poor copy from a black-and-white copier that appears muddy.

Rubber-Stamping and Related Techniques

With the increasing popularity of paper crafts, rubber-stamping and related techniques have become popular for creating designs and special effects. You are limited only by your imagination.

Brayering
A brayer is used to create interesting backgrounds on paper. Try using a

variegated or rainbow ink pad, *bottom right*, for creating colorful backgrounds.

Getting started: To make stripes and plaids, use felt-tip markers to draw color bands of various widths and designs on a brayer for out-of-the-ordinary backgrounds. Design plaids by rolling various colors in one direction on a sheet of paper, then applying colors in the opposite direction.

Create ghost images by first stamping the paper with embossing ink, then loading the brayer with dye-based ink, and rolling it over the stamped paper. The images will subtly appear in the background. If desired, use the same rubber stamp and embossing powder on top of the ghost images to give the paper dimension and shine.

Coloring Stamped Images *(not shown)*
Two popular options for filling in stamped images are watercolor pencils and felt-tip

The photo at left was taken with a traditional on-camera flash. With the aid of a waxed-paper-wrapped flashlight shining inside the pumpkin and a second wrapped flashlight shining below the trick-or-treater's face, the photo becomes much more dramatic, as shown above.

markers. Watercolor pencils can be tricky but are worth the time spent learning to use them because they create beautiful results. Follow the manufacturer's instructions for specific techniques.

Creating Dimension (not shown)
Give dimension to your paper crafts by cutting stamped images out of card stock, then attaching the image to a greeting card or other project with double-sided foam adhesive dots or squares.

Heat Embossing – *See Embossing, page 11.*

Glittering (above left)
Use glitter to give your paper crafts extra sparkle for the holidays and special occasions. When the stamped image is dry, apply adhesive with a glue pen following the outline of the image. Sprinkle the glitter on the wet glue. Let the glue dry; then tap the excess off the image and return it to the original container.

Inking with Brush-Type Markers
(not shown)
Brush-type markers allow for exact control of color placement on specific areas of the stamp.

Apply the marker ink using the broad tip and blend the color directly on the surface of the rubber stamp. For smooth color gradations, apply the ink to the stamp with various markers, beginning with the lightest; then go back over any lines where the colors meet with the lighter color. If the ink seems to have dried before the image is stamped, use a light breath (similar to cleaning eyeglasses) on the stamp to remoisten the ink and then stamp with firm, even pressure.

Inking with Stamp Pads (left)
Although inking a stamp may seem simple, take care when applying the ink so that a perfect image will be created each time you stamp. Too little ink will create faint lines or only a partial imprint and too much ink will cause blurred lines.

If you've been disappointed by the darkness of a stamped image for a background, try the new watermark stamp pad for stamping lighter images.

Instead of trying to find a sticker vase, the designer cut a section from a wrought-iron fence border, above, *to make her own container for the buds to sit in.*

A sticker bow layered on top of the tulip stalks finishes the look, above.

Press or rub the stamp on the ink pad several times until the rubber die is completely inked. Then apply a steady, even pressure as the stamp is applied to the paper surface. To prevent mistakes, the stamp should not be rocked and should be lifted straight up from the surface.

Suede Paper Embossing – *See Embossing, page 11.*

Using Stickers

Creative Cutting *(opposite center)*

Another option with stickers is to think beyond the original design purpose. If the sticker design isn't quite what you had in mind, a little creative snipping, as shown with the tulips, can make it perfect.

Layering *(above)*

Combine multiple stickers on top of each other to create a scene that is much more interesting than a single sticker. Look for stickers that have similar color intensities and hues, and proportions that work well together. For the card shown, the Easter egg sticker was placed on top of a decorative-block sticker and the edge of the flap was accented with a coordinating rickrack border.

Powdering *(center right)*

Using baby powder or cornstarch, you can eliminate the tackiness of the adhesive on sticker, allowing the sticker to be used as a photo corners or even a photo pocket. The top edge of the wave sticker was powdered to create a photo pocket. The photo will remain undamaged by the sticker, allowing the picture to be easily removed later if desired.

Splicing *(right)*

Use border stickers along the sides to lend a finished look to a photo. The secret to a

To make photo corners and a pocket from a sticker, leave the parts of the sticker that are to stick to the page tacky and powder the rest. The photo will slide safely into the powdered areas, above.

well-made border is in the cutting of the corners. Instead of cutting a straight edge on the end of each border sticker strip, cut one pair of opposite-lying border strips at a mitered angle. When the sticker borders are placed on the photo, the effect will be that all corners have been mitered without the need to make precision cuts on all the pieces.

To powder a sticker, dip a small paintbrush into a shallow dish of baby powder and brush the powder onto the back of the sticker where no stickiness is desired.

Lettering Techniques

Garden Style

Just perfect for your spring and summer projects, this shaded and embellished garden alphabet uses a technique called color layering. The method uses the gradual transition of colors to add depth and definition to the letters. Scroll and brush markers create fast, fun, and dramatic letter and floral embellishments on pages, book covers, and note cards.

Whether you're making a wedding album, a graduation scrapbook page, or a baby card, garden-style lettering adds a delicate touch to the message with tiny nosegays sprinkled among the letters.

Making the Letters

1. Trace the letters on tracing paper and lightly transfer the lettering to the project.

2. Use brush- and fine-tip markers to color and shade the letters. To make the flowers, place the brush tip of the marker as flat to the paper as possible and gently press, forming a tear-drop shape. Keep your brush tip in for the petals and out for the leaves.

—*Designed by Susy Ratto*

Create elegant thank-you notes and bridal shower invitations with shaded garden-style lettering.

1

2

3

4

Materials
Baby Shower Gift Bag
- Denim paper gift bag, medium size
- Card stock: yellow polka dot, light pink, and white
- Corrugated paper: green and yellow
- Die cuts: baby rattle and duck (from the Natural Baby die-cut pack)
- Double-sided foam-adhesive dots
- Glue stick
- Pinking shears
- Hole punch
- Decorative diaper pin
- ⅓ yard of 1"-wide sheer blue ribbon

Baby Shower Gift Bag
Rattled for a baby shower wrap? Use a fancy diaper pin to attach this toy-trimmed tag to the gift bag. **Note:** *See* page 31 *for instructions to make the plaid shower invitation shown* above.

Instructions
1. Use a pinking shears to cut a rectangle from the yellow polka-dot paper large enough to accommodate the rattle die cut. Mount the yellow rectangle on white card stock with the glue stick. Trim the white card stock about ¼" beyond the edges of the yellow rectangle.

2. Die cut the rattle out of green corrugated paper and the duck out of yellow. Cut a strip of light pink card stock to fit across the rattle and on the handle. Mount the strip on the rattle with foam-adhesive dots. Glue the pink paper to the handle. Tie a ribbon bow to the handle at the base of the rattle, and trim ends at an angle. Use the hole punch to make a hole near the edge of the duck's head. Write "To:" and "From:" on the back of the duck's body. To attach the duck, cut a small slit in the handle and push the duck onto the handle. Mount the rattle on the yellow rectangle with adhesive dots.

3. Position the gift tag on the front of the gift bag. Pin the top center of the gift tag to the bag with the diaper pin. Fill the bag with tissue paper and insert the gift.

—*Designed by Heather Mason*

Baby Ducks Gift Bag

Unmistakable signs hang from a border of floating ducks on this gift bag for a baby. The bag, which will be cherished for your thoughtfulness, is cute enough to be a greeting card.

Instructions

1. Cut and use spray adhesive to adhere the polka-dot paper to the bag. Cut a strip from the duck paper to trim the bag. Punch two small holes in the lower portion of the strip, spacing each hole about 1½" from the edge of the paper. Place glue only across the upper edge of the strip, leaving the lower portion free.

2. Cut and adhere additional border strips to the bottom of the bag. Cut a duck out of the paper and mount on the white card stock, then on blue polka-dot paper cut ¼" larger than the white. Mount on the borders at the bottom of the bag.

3. Cut a square and a rectangle from the white card stock. Using the black marker, write "for" and "baby," and then draw long dashed lines on the cards. Punch holes in the upper corners of the signs.

4. Tie a knot in one end of the twine. Thread the twine through one corner hole in the sign, through the hole in the border, and then the other corner hole, ending with a knot.

—*Designed by Polly McMillan*

Materials

Baby Ducks Gift Bag
- Mini brown paper gift bag
- White card stock
- Blue polka-dot paper
- Printworks duck paper
- Small hole punch
- Wide-tip black marker
- Spray adhesive
- Glue stick
- Fine twine

Years from now you will look back at this album and remember the special moments captured in this precious baby book.

Materials
Sweet Dreams Album
- Post-bound scrapbook with 8½×11" pages
- 2 varieties of embossed white paper
- Mulberry paper: blue or pink, and yellow
- Paper: blue or pink
- Yellow star-motif background paper
- 1⅛"-tall letter stencil
- Three ¾" wooden stars
- Yellow acrylic paint
- Paintbrush
- Fine-tip black marker
- Acid-free adhesive
- Double-sided tape
- Drill and small bit
- Yellow embroidery floss
- 8" of ½"-wide sheer blue ribbon

Sweet Dreams Album
Save the precious moments of your baby's first year in this priceless moon and stars album you will always cherish.

Instructions
1. Remove the album posts and take the album apart. Use blue or pink mulberry paper and double-sided tape to cover the front and back. Put the album back together.

2. To make layered letter blocks, cut four 1¾" squares from the embossed white papers. From the blue (or pink) paper, cut four squares about ⅛" larger than the white squares. From the yellow mulberry paper, tear four 2¾" squares. Use double-sided tape to attach the layers. Use the letter stencil and a fine-tip black marking pen to trace "BABY" letters onto the blue or pink paper; cut out the letters just beyond the traced lines. Adhere the letters to the layered blocks.

3. Drill a small hole through one point of each wooden star. Paint the wooden stars yellow; let the paint dry. From yellow embroidery floss, cut three lengths of floss varying in length from 6" to 8". Insert a length of thread through the hole in each star; bring ends of thread together.

4. From embossed white paper, cut a 6" tall crescent moon. Use a black marker to outline the moon just inside the cut edges. To attach the wooden stars, cut a small slit in the moon, referring to the photo *above* for placement. Insert the thread ends through the slit from front to back; secure ends to the back of moon with double-sided tape. Wrap the sheer ribbon around the white moon and tie in a bow, covering the hole; secure with tape. Adhere the white moon to a piece of yellow mulberry paper with tape; tear the yellow paper about ½" beyond the yellow moon.

5. Adhere the letter blocks and the moon to the front of the album with double-sided tape. Cut small stars from star-motif paper; glue randomly to the album cover.

—Designed by Roberta Roys

Baby Brett's Page

Use stickers to avoid misdrawn characters and errant ink marks. Brett's mom used them on his baby page to letter his name and to trim the bottle, photo, and date.

Instructions

1. Mount the photo on white paper with adhesive. Trim the white paper about ¼" beyond the edges of the photo. Use a blue marking pen to draw a dashed line along the edges of the white paper. Mount the white paper on the baby motif patterned paper. Trim the patterned paper ½" beyond the edges of the white paper. Add a sticker to the bottom left corner if desired.

2. From the white paper with blue dots, cut a square large enough to accommodate your alphabet stickers for each letter of the baby's name plus a small baby motif-sticker. Draw a dash-and-dot line around the edges of each of the squares, using a dark blue marker for the letter squares and a light green marker for the motif square. Press the stickers onto the squares.

3. To make layered blocks, cut squares from one of the blue papers about ⅜" larger than the sticker squares. From the remaining blue paper, cut squares about ¼" larger than the first blue squares. Layer the blue squares and then mount the sticker squares at various angles on the top blue square.

4. From the baby motif paper, cut a narrow rectangle about 5½" to 6" long for the bottom of the page. From the white, light blue, and dark blue papers, cut squares for mounting. Place the duck sticker on the white square. Use a blue marker to add a border to the top light blue square of the layered motif block. Mount the papers together; then mount the motif block centered on the rectangle with double-sided foam-adhesive dots.

5. From the light blue paper, die-cut a baby bottle. Apply a floral sticker to the baby bottle die cut. Use markers to color and add detail to the bottle.

6. Arrange the layered pieces and the bottle die cut on the sheet of blue card stock. When you are pleased with the arrangement, attach the layered pieces with adhesive and the die cut with double-sided foam adhesive dots. Use a blue pen to write the date at the bottom of the page. Mount on the album page.

—Designed by Vickie Breslin

Materials

Baby Brett's Page

- Baby photo
- Archival-quality photo album page
- 8½×11" sheet of blue card stock
- Paper: white and two shades of blue
- Patterned paper: blue-and-white baby motif and white with blue dots
- Baby bottle die cut
- Stickers: alphabet, floral, and baby motifs (duck)
- Brush- and fine-tip markers: dark blue and green
- Acid-free adhesive
- Double-sided foam-adhesive dots

birthday
greetings

Happy Birthday

Materials
A Pocketful of Birthday Wishes
- Birthday photo(s)
- 8½×11" archival-quality album page
- Card stock: assorted colors for flowers and leaves
- Acid-free paper: hot pink, medium pink, and white
- Small vellum envelope
- Flower and leaf die-cuts
- Birthday cake sticker
- Assorted brush- and fine-tip markers
- Acid-free adhesive

A Pocketful of Birthday Wishes

A pocketful of pictures and party wishes keeps this day forever young. Line an envelope with pink paper; then decorate with paper flowers and a photo.

Instructions

1. From the medium pink paper, cut a shape to line the envelope. Adhere the liner inside the envelope using the acid-free adhesive.

2. Cut a rectangle from the white paper. Use a marking pen to write the person's name and special occasion on the rectangle. Mount the white rectangle on a medium pink paper. Center and trim the paper about ½" beyond the edges of the white paper.

3. From the card stock, cut assorted flowers and leaves with the die cuts.

4. Arrange the envelope, layered rectangles, and flower die cuts on an 8½×11" sheet of hot pink paper, then adhere the pieces to the paper. Make swirls on the page and a flower design on the envelope using the markers. Add outlines along the edges of the layered rectangles and dashed lines on the envelope.

5. Cut a small square from the white and medium pink papers. Use a marking pen to decorate the edges of the white square with a line border. Mount the white square on the center of the envelope. Mount the pink square with the corners in the opposite direction from the corners of the white square. Press a birthday cake sticker onto the pink square. Use marking pens to add a message on the envelope. Slip the photo(s) into the envelope. Adhere the layered papers to the album page.

—*Designed by Lindsay Ostrom*

Materials

Happy Birthday Buckle
- 5×6½" blank white card
- Paper Flair items as follows:
  - Pink Petite Prints Paper Pack
  - Pastel Vellum Paper Pack
  - Painted Vellum Card Embellishments: birthday cake motif
- Liquid adhesive
- Spray adhesive
- 9" length of ¼"-wide light pink sheer ribbon

Happy Birthday Buckle

Using swirl paper in two shades of pink, create an elegant birthday card held together with a fancy birthday cake buckle.

Instructions

1. Cut 2½" from the right opening edge of the card front, and reserve the excess card stock. Using spray adhesive, adhere the light pink swirls paper to the remaining card front. Cover the inside back with the dark pink swirls paper.

2. Glue a ⅜×6½" rectangular strip of the dark pink swirls paper to the left side of the card front next to the fold, and the same size strip of the light pink swirls paper to the right edge of the inside back.

3. Cut out the birthday cake vellum embellishment and mat on pink striped paper, trimming the edges to a ¼" border.

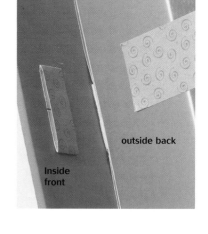

Cut a 1½×3¾" piece each of the light and dark pink swirls paper. Adhere the pieces vertically side-by-side to the center of a 3½×4¼" piece of dark pink vellum.

4. *To make the strap:* Cut a ¾×2½" strip from dark pink swirls paper and a ¾×3" strip from light pink swirls paper. Glue each to the reserved card piece for strength and trim along the edges of the paper strips. Glue the dark pink swirl strip horizontally across the left center of the card front. Glue the left half of the matted cake embellishment to the right edge of the card front, centered over the card front and inside back.

5. *To make the buckle:* Fold back 1" of one end of the light pink swirls strap; then glue that end to the back of the card, making sure the remainder of the strap overlaps the front and is centered across from the left-hand strap. Cut a ½×2⅛" strip of light pink swirls paper and fold each end ½" toward the back to make the buckle. Insert the left end of the light pink strap through the small folded buckle and adhere the buckle to the back of the matted cake embellishment. Tie a bow and glue it to the front of the card as shown.

—Designed by Susan Cobb

Accordion-Fold Birthday Card

"Accordion" to this card, someone turns one year old today! Even in this no-frills, easy-cut version, the paper letters dance across the folds with wishes for the best birthday ever.

Instructions

1. Cut two 2¾×12" strips from My Stars paper. Using spray adhesive, adhere the strips together, overlapping them ¼" along a short edge. Mark and accordion-fold the strip at 2⅜" intervals. Trim excess paper.

2. Cut one 1¼×1⅝" rectangle from each of the Pretty Pink papers. Trace the letters on *page 88* with tracing paper, transfer to the Pretty Pink papers, and cut out the letters for BIRTHDAY.

3. Using the decorative-edge scissors, cut ten 1⅝×2⅛" off-white card stock rectangles. Apply a sticker to one, write a birthday message on one, and glue letters to the remainder. Adhere the rectangles to the folded strip with double-sided tape. Tie a ribbon around the card.

Materials

Accordion-Fold Birthday Card

- Off-white card stock
- Ever After Papers in Mountain Pine, My Stars, and Pretty Pink patterns: My Stars, Spiral, Ticking Stripe, Small Check, Country Check, Grass, Basket Weave, and Vine
- Debbie Mumm Collectors' Happy Birthday sticker
- Fine-tip black marking pen
- Decorative-edge scallop scissors
- Double-sided tape
- Spray adhesive
- Tracing paper
- ½ yard of ⅝"-wide pink organdy ribbon

Let's Party

Think of the tiny package on the front of this birthday card as the prelude to a special day filled with good things.

Instructions

1. Cut a 3⅞×5⅛" rectangle from the white card stock. Cut thin strips of the light blue and light green vellum with the decorative-edge scissors. Glue the strips to the white rectangle. Attach the rectangle to the pink note card with the photo corners.

2. *To make the package:* Cut the mat board into a 2½" square. Randomly place the stickers on one side of the mat board. Wrap the square with the pink vellum and stamp the front of the vellum with the jade ink. Tie the ribbon around the package and make a bow. Adhere the package to the front of the card with double-sided tape.

3. *To make the tag:* Attach a party sticker to a small piece of the white card stock. Punch a hole in the upper left corner. Attach the tag to the package with the gold cord.

—*Designed by Stephanie Scheetz*

Materials

Let's Party
- 4¼×5½" pink note card
- White card stock
- Vellum: light blue, light green, and pink
- White mat board
- PSX items as follows:
  - Birthday Sticker sheet
  - Brushy Favorites Pixie rubber-stamp set
- Pearlescent Jade Brilliance ink pad
- Gold photo corners
- Decorative-edge scissors
- ⅛" hole punch
- Double-sided foam tape
- Liquid adhesive
- ⅜" wide sheer mint green ribbon
- Gold cord

Cut and curl a brightly colored assortment of edged strips to form a fanciful "ribbon" bow on a gift package.

Materials

Gift Package
- White paper box
- Paper: yellow, hot pink, orange, and lime green
- Assorted decorative-edge scissors
- Double-sided tape

Fringed Place Mat and Hat
- 8½×12" card stock: yellow, hot pink, orange, purple, and lime green
- 8½×12" paper: yellow, hot pink, orange, purple, and lime green
- 12×16" patterned papers: blue with white dots and yellow with gold stars
- Ellison Craft & Design die-cuts: party, gift, streamers, party hat, and party favor
- Assorted decorative-edge scissors
- Xyron laminating machine
- Double-sided tape
- Liquid adhesive

Paper Fringe

Make bright and festive party decorations, hats, and gift packages with colorful papers and fringe made using decorative-edge scissors.

Instructions

Gift Package

1. For the ribbon around the package, use a wide decorative-edge-cut strip and cut ¾"-wide slits at ½" intervals along the entire length. The slits allow for a narrower, contrasting strip to be woven through the first. Wrap around the package and secure with tape.

2. *To make the bow:* Using a variety of decorative-edge scissors, cut an assortment of narrow and wide strips from hot pink, orange, lime green, and yellow paper. Wrap the strips around a pencil to form loops. Tuck the ends of the loops under the ribbon on the package and secure with double-sided tape.

Place Mat

1. Using the party die cuts, cut the designs from the card stock, arrange and adhere onto the yellow with gold stars paper; then adhere the yellow paper to the blue with white dots paper. Laminate the paper using the Xyron laminating machine.

2. Using five different colors of paper, cut 2"-wide strips to fit around all four sides of the laminated sheet. Using decorative-edge scissors, make 1½"-long cuts into the sides of each strip. Layer and adhere all five colors of fringe on the back of the place mat with tape and fluff the fringe.

Hat

1. Roll a piece of blue paper with white dots into a cone shape and tape closed with double-sided tape. Trim the bottom even and cut a small opening in the tip of the cone.

2. Using five colors of paper, cut 2"-wide strips from each piece and make 1¼"-long cuts into each side (like the fringe on the place mat). Layer the colors together with double-sided tape, fluff the fringe, and tape to the bottom of the hat.

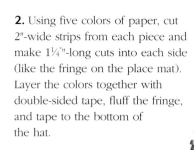

3. To make the pom-pom, cut 4×5" strips from five colors of paper. Using decorative-edge scissors, make cuts (like the fringe on the place mat) without cutting all the way through the strip. Layer the pieces and lightly roll together to make the pom-pom. Wrap tape around the uncut end to secure. Insert pom-pom into small opening in the top of the hat and apply a little glue around the opening.

—Designed by Shannon Smith

Materials
Birthday Wishes Gift Bag
- 8×10½" yellow gift bag
- Flower print tissue paper
- 2¼×4¼" white tag
- Flower die cuts
- Brush- and fine-tip markers
- Double-sided foam-adhesive dots
- Liquid adhesive
- 7" length of 1½"-wide polka-dot ribbon

A Tower of Flower Power
- 3 same-size gift boxes
- Tissue paper: yellow, orange, and pink
- Flower die cuts
- Liquid adhesive
- Several yards of 3"-wide sheer pink ribbon

Flower Power
Use flowers and colorful tags to embellish these gifts. A plain yellow bag gets a jolt of summer with its floral accents, and a tower of packages is tied with bright pink ribbon scattered with stylized blossoms.

Birthday Wishes Gift Bag
Instructions
1. Use a purple marker to draw a border around the front edges of the white tag. Use markers to write the birthday message and to draw a variety of dots on the tag. Thread the ribbon through the hole in the tag, and tie a knot.

2. Arrange the finished tag and the flower die cuts on the front of the gift bag. When

you are pleased with the arrangement, adhere the pieces to the bag, using glue or double-sided foam-adhesive dots to add dimension. Fill the bag with tissue paper and insert the gift.

A Tower of Flower Power
Instructions
1. Wrap each gift box with a different color of tissue paper. Glue flower die cuts to the sides of the boxes, covering the folded paper ends.

2. Stack the wrapped boxes and tie the sheer ribbon in a bow around the boxes. Add flower die cuts to the ribbon tails.
—Designed by Shannon Smith

Birthday Flowers

Make these boldly colored flowers to add even more fun to your birthday party. Use in flower containers with florist's foam in the bottom to secure the flowers. Add natural excelsior to cover the foam.

Instructions

1. Trace the patterns on *pages 92–93*, making one for each of the petal sets (three), and the leaf. Cut out the patterns.

2. Cut a 6" square from one print paper, a ?" square from another, and a 2½" square from the third. Fold each square in quarters. Trace the petal patterns on the appropriate folded squares and cut them out. Open up the petals; then fold them in quarters on the

diagonal. Open up the petals. Layer the petals from small to large; and glue together with hotmelt adhesive. Add the pom-pom in the center.

3. From the green and white striped paper, cut two leaves, reversing one. Glue the leaves together, sandwiching half of one length of florist's wire in between.

4. Fold the remaining length of the florist's wire in half, forming a loop. Completely wrap the dowel with the florist's tape, catching the leaf and then the wire loop at the top of the dowel, leaving ¼" of the loop exposed. Glue the flowers to the dowel.

—Designed by Keri Schneider

Materials

Birthday Flowers
- Patterns on pages 92–93
- 3 each of assorted papers per flower: ladybugs, red flowers on blue, daisies and hearts, yellow and white stripes, red and white dots, and multicolor stripes
- 2 each of green and white stripe paper
- Spray adhesive
- Tracing paper
- Glue gun and hotmelt adhesive
- Two 6" lengths of florist's wire
- ³/₁₆"-diameter dowel
- Green florist's tape
- Brass fasteners
- 2"-diameter yellow pom-poms

SIERRA

academic
milestones

CONGRAD"U"ATIONS

ABC

Alta Dutch Flat Elementary School

8th Grade
Graduation
D.L.S.

Katie
June 1996
and Christi

Christi
June 1998
and Katie

ommemorate
the momentous
academic milestones
—at every age and
for every degree of
accomplishment.
Make the graduate
feel special with a
handmade tribute.

Graduation Gift Boxes

Instructions

1. Paint the cardboard and the box green (or any desired color) using the sponge brush. Let dry and paint a second coat if needed. Paint the inside of the box and the head of the fastener black. Paint the box lid black inside and out. Let dry.

2. Glue the top of the box lid to the center of the painted cardboard square. Using an awl, pierce a small hole in the top center of the lid and the square.

3. Insert the painted fastener through the lid from the outside to the inside. Loop the tassel around the head of the fastener.

Firmly press the fastener in place and spread the prongs apart.

4. Finish the round box by painting stripes or dots. Paint black stripes with a fine-line brush. Paint dots by dipping the handle end of a paintbrush or a pencil eraser into paint and dotting onto the surface.

—*Designed by Sue Banker*

Materials

Graduation Gift Boxes

- 4"-square piece of cardboard
- 2¾"-diameter round papier-mâché box with lid
- Acrylic paints: green and black, or other desired color combination
- Artist's fine-line paintbrush
- Sponge brush
- Brass fastener
- Liquid adhesive
- Tassel: black or desired color
- Awl

Trim the pink paper about ⅛" beyond the side and top edges of the pictures. Plan the amount of space needed for the name and trim the pink paper below the photos. Mount the pink paper on white paper. Trim the white paper about ⅛" beyond the edges of the pink paper.

3. Mount a sheet of floral pattern paper on a white photo album page; then mount the layered 12 years of photos centered on the floral paper. Use the leaf punch to make two or three leaves from the green paper for each flower letter. Arrange the leaves and flower letters on the pink paper below the photos. Attach the leaves with adhesive and the flower letters with double-sided foam adhesive dots. Adhere to a photo album page.

All Grown Up!
1. Use the computer, printer, and white paper to make a grid corresponding to the school photos, showing the year, grade, and age of the graduate in each photo. Also make a box on white paper and journal in the box about the graduate. Trim along the outside of each box.

2. Use the circle punch to make 11 circles from white paper. Use the second set of alphabet stickers to spell "All Grown Up!" on the white circles. Mount the circles on pink paper. Trim the pink paper into a rectangle around the letters.

3. Trim some of the photos around the graduate, eliminating the background. Referring to the page *opposite* for ideas, mount the photos, grid, journal box, and lettered rectangle on a variety of solid and patterned papers. Trim the papers, creating a ⅛" to ½"-wide paper border. Add as many layers of paper as desired, varying the width of the borders.

4. Arrange the layered pieces on the second white photo album page. When you are pleased with the arrangement, adhere the pieces to the page. Use a fine-tip black marking pen to write additional information. Cut out individual flowers from the floral patterned paper and mount with foam adhesive dots.

—Designed by Arlene Santo

Materials
School Pictures and All Grown Up!
- Assorted photos, including 12 years of school photos
- Two 12" square archival-quality photo album pages
- Papers: 3 pink, 2 white, and 2 green
- Patterned paper: 2 floral and 1 blue with white polka dots
- 2 varieties of alphabet stickers
- Punches: flower, leaf, and circle
- Fine-point black marking pen
- Double-sided tape
- Double-sided foam-adhesive dots
- Acid-free adhesive
- Microsoft Chaucer computer font
- Computer, printer, and acid-free paper

Through the Years
Gather the graduate's small school portraits and create a scrapbook page that shows the amazing growing years from first grade through high school graduation.

Instructions
School Pictures
1. To make layered flower letters, use the flower punch and pink paper to make a flower for each letter of the graduate's name. Press the sticker letters onto the pink flowers. Mount the pink flowers on white paper with double-stick tape. Trim the white paper just beyond the edges of the pink flowers to create a narrow border. Mount the white flowers on the blue patterned paper. Trim the patterned paper about ⅛" beyond the edges of the white flowers.

2. Trim the school photos from grades 1 through 12 all to the same size. Arrange them in three rows of four photos on the pink paper, leaving an even amount of space between the photos and the rows. Adhere the photos with double-sided tape.

ALL GROWN UP!

1989 1st Grade age 6	1990 2nd Grade age 7	1991 3rd Grade age 8	1992 4th Grade age 9
1993 5th Grade age 10	1994 6th Grade age 11	1995 7th Grade age 12	1996 8th Grade age 13
1997 9th Grade age 14	1998 10th Grade age 15	1999 11th Grade age 16	Class of 2000 12th Grade age 17

"1983" Sierra age 1 & Debbie age 23

"2000" Sierra age 17 & Debbie age 39

Sierra Santos-Griffiths, my niece
all grown up! It seems like yesterday
at she was a baby in Debbie's arms (my
ter). And now, it is the year 2000, and
rra has graduated from High School.
future is bright with promise as she
's into the new millenium. You go girl!

A college graduate will appreciate a fun, brightly colored page as much as a younger child. Tuck an extra photo or a reduced copy of the diploma into the pocket for a clever touch.

Materials
Con"grad"uations
- Graduation photo
- 8½×11" archival-quality album page
- Paper: black, yellow, and white
- Die cuts: pocket, apple, and ABC letters
- Reduced photocopy of diploma
- Assorted marking pens
- Acid-free adhesive

Con"grad"uations

This page is a big success—whatever the graduate's age! Reduce a college diploma on a photocopier and fit it into the pocket for added dimension. To celebrate a younger child's accomplishment, slip a report card or other award inside.

Instructions

1. Trim the photo into a rectangle, noting how the cap extends beyond one edge of the rectangle. Mount the trimmed photo on white paper with adhesive. Trim the white paper about ⅛" beyond the edges of the photo. Use a marking pen to draw a dash-and-dot border on the white paper. Mount the white rectangle on yellow paper, and trim the yellow paper about ¼" beyond the edges of the white rectangle.

2. Cut a long rectangle from white paper to fit across the top of the page. Use a black marking pen to write CON"GRAD"UATIONS in block letters on the white rectangle, referring to the photo at *left* for ideas. Color in the letters with marking pens. Decorate the rectangle with large dots and add a dash-and-dot border along the edges. Mount the white rectangle on yellow paper. Trim the yellow paper about ¼" beyond the edges of the white rectangle.

3. Mount the apple die cut on the pocket die cut. Use a white marking pen to add dashed lines along the stitch lines of the pocket and to outline the apple. Use various colors to outline along the edges of the ABC letters.

4. Trim a second sheet of white paper to measure 8×10½". Mount the trimmed white sheet centered on a sheet of black paper. Draw a black dashed line along the edges of the white paper. Arrange the layered pieces and the die cuts on the white sheet. When you are pleased with the arrangement, attach the side and bottom edges of the pocket to the paper, leaving the top edge open. Adhere the remaining pieces to the paper. Slip the diploma photocopy into the pocket. Adhere the layered papers to the album page.

—Designed by Lindsay Ostrom and Vickie Breslin

Graduation Artistry

No patterned papers, fancy scissors, paper punches, or extra trims here. This spectacular album page is done entirely with marking pens.

Materials
Eighth-Grade Graduation
- Graduation photos
- 8½×11" archival-quality photo album page
- Assorted brush- and fine-tip markers
- Double-sided tape
- Pencil

Eighth-Grade Graduation

Refer to *pages 16–17* in *Paper Craft Basics* to create beautifully shaded garden-style lettering. There, you'll also find a pattern for all the letters so you can create a similar page for your own scrapbook.

Instructions

1. Plan for the placement of the lettering by first arranging the photos on the photo album page. Use a pencil to lightly draw borders around the photos. Set the photos aside; then use the brush-tip markers to color the designs.

2. Use the brush-tip markers for lettering, flowers, leaves, and the page border. Use the fine-tip markers for outlining and detail lettering.

3. Mount the photos on the page with double-sided tape.

—Designed by Susy Ratto

springsummer
celebrations

*S*how friends and family how much you care when you make handmade cards with personalized sentiments, gift bags for presents, and scrapbook pages that preserve holiday photos you'll always cherish.

Materials

Red Roses Valentine Card
- 5×6½" blank white card
- Paper: gold metallic and pale yellow
- Hot Off the Press papers:
  - Red Roses paper
  - Lace and Dot vellum
- Heart template
- Spray adhesive
- Liquid adhesive
- Metallic gold marking pen
- Gold thread

Red Roses Valentine Card

So simple and so elegant—give this red rose and lace Valentine's Day card to the special person in your life.

Instructions

1. Cut the Red Roses paper to fit the front of the card. Spray the Red Roses paper with spray adhesive and cover the front of the card with the paper.

2. Cut the Lace and Dot vellum to wrap around the outside of the card, overlapping the lace borders at the center front. Use spray adhesive to adhere the vellum to the back of the card.

3. Cut out a 1⅜" square from the Red Roses paper and double-mat it on pale yellow and metallic gold paper. Turn the square on end to make a diamond shape and glue it to the center of the left vellum flap.

4. Cover the inside of the card with pale yellow paper. Double-mat a heart cut from

Red Roses paper on pale yellow and metallic gold paper; then glue it to the inside center of the card.

5. Tie a bow using the gold thread and glue it to the top of the heart. Add journaling with the metallic gold marking pen.

—*Designed by Susan Cobb*

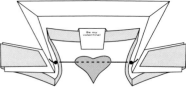

Materials

Be My Valentine
- White card stock
- Pink check vellum
- White vellum
- Paper Reflections heart die cut
- Black marking pen
- Liquid adhesive
- Ivory cotton thread
- Large needle

Be My Valentine

It's okay to leave the recipient of this Valentine card hanging—when the double door is pulled open, the suspended thread raises the pretty vellum heart.

Note: *You can turn almost any object into a dangling centerpiece with a clothesline pop-up card.*

Instructions

1. Cut a 5½×10¾" rectangle from the white card stock. Referring to *Diagram A* on *page 89* and the *Folding and Construction Diagram above right*, mark, score, and fold the white paper.

2. Cut a 4¾×10½" rectangle from the pink check vellum. Referring to *Diagram B* on *page 89*, and the *Folding and Construction*

Folding and Construction Diagram

Diagram above, mark, score and fold the lines as indicated. Glue the white and pink papers together at the folded ends as indicated with a C, *above*. Cut a small white vellum rectangle, write a message, sign your name, and adhere to the card.

3. Cut a 5" length of cotton thread. Make tiny holes with the needle as indicated in the *Construction Diagram*. Knot the thread, pull through both holes and knot on the other end. Glue the heart to the thread.

-Designed by Jean Wilson

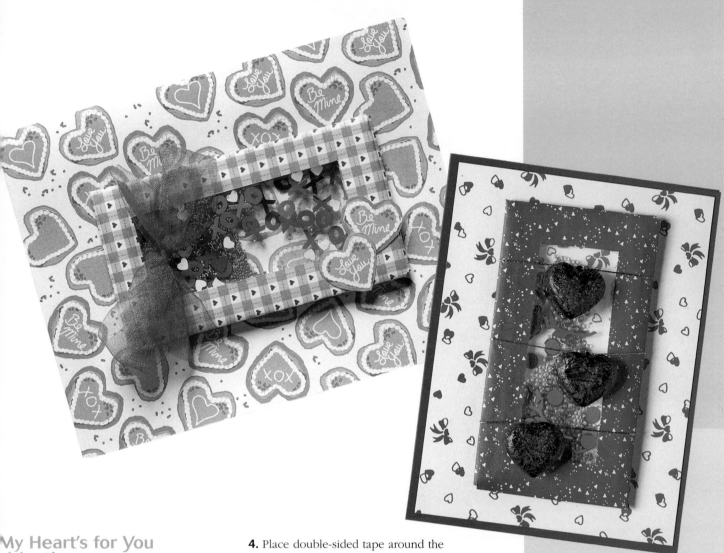

My Heart's for You Valentines

Give your heart to the valentine in your life with a handmade card expressing sweet sentiments of love.

Instructions

1. From the card stock, cut one 5½×10" rectangle for a large card or one 5½×8½" rectangle for a small card; fold the rectangle in half. Cut a piece of decorative paper the same size or ¼" to ½" smaller than the folded card; use spray adhesive to adhere it to the card front.

2. To make a shaker frame, stamp the template image on the back side of the paper selected for the frame. Use a crafts knife to score the card stock on the dotted lines (fold lines for flaps), and cut on the solid lines.

3. Measure the window opening adding ¼" to the length and width; then cut a piece of clear plastic for the window.

4. Place double-sided tape around the underside edge of the window opening; secure the clear plastic to the frame to create the window. Place a double layer of foam tape end to end on the underside of the frame on the outside edges, being careful not to leave any gaps. Using two layers of tape will allow the confetti to move around inside the window. Holding the frame upside down, fill the area inside the foam tape with confetti or other filler.

5. Fold in the four frame flaps; place double-sided tape on the outside of the flaps. Tie ribbon in a bow around the shaker or wrap decorative thread with heart charms around the shaker. Center and adhere the assembled shaker to the card front.

—Designed by Holly Springer

Materials

My Heart's for You Valentine
- Card stock
- Card stock or lighter weight paper (for shaker)
- Valentine decorative paper
- Rubber-stamp shaker template: Art Gone Wild X3-1208 or X3-1209
- Quick-drying ink pad
- Clear window plastic
- Double-sided tape
- Double-sided foam-adhesive tape
- Spray adhesive
- Crafts knife
- Confetti and/or filler such as tiny glass beads, glitter, shells, buttons, etc.
- Decorative threads and heart charms or ribbon

Materials

For the Paper-Cast:
- Bathroom tissue
- Rubber stamp with a simple design
- Dry towel
- Pearl Ex, colored chalk, stencil paint, or other dry or semidry pigmented mediums

Easy Paper-Cast Cards

Pastel cards with bunnies and eggs are welcome reminders that spring has sprung and it's time to celebrate Easter.

Instructions

Making the Paper-Cast

1. Make a stack of about 10 squares of bathroom tissue. Moisten the paper in the sink and gently press against the side of the sink to remove excess water.

2. Place a clean rubber stamp faceup on your work surface. Press the wet paper directly onto the stamp, using your fingers to push the paper into the details.

3. While the paper is wet, tear the sides to form the deckle edges; the side of the stamp serves as a straightedge (see *Step 1, opposite*).

4. Using a dry towel, press more excess water from the paper, moving to a dry section of the towel when one section becomes damp. Carefully remove the paper-cast image from the surface of the stamp and set it aside to dry.

5. When dry, color the image with Pearl Ex, colored chalk, stencil paint, or other paint medium (see *Step 2, opposite*).

Step 1

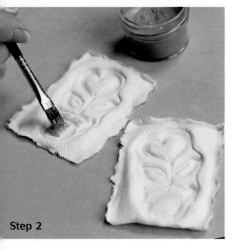

Step 2

6. When using a multiple-image stamp, the entire paper-cast can be used on the card or torn apart to make individual images. Moisten dry edges with a wet paintbrush before tearing.

Making the Card
1. Cut a rectangle of card stock; fold the card stock in half using a creasing tool. Cut smaller pieces of coordinating papers and adhere them to the card stock with double-sided tape (or use foam-adhesive tape to add dimension).

2. Attach the paper-cast image with double-sided tape or foam tape. Embellish the card with ribbon, if desired. **Note:** *Liquid adhesive will cause the layers to separate.*

—Designed by Holly Springer

Materials
For the Card:
- Card stock
- Papers in pastel colors
- Rubber stamps:
  flowerpot, chicks, bunnies,
  and Easter egg
- Creasing tool
- Double-sided tape or
  foam-adhesive tape
- Assorted ribbons

Materials

Hatched Chick Easter Surprise

- Cream card stock
- Paper: yellow with large polka dots and blue with small white polka dots
- Egg die cuts
- Decorative-edge scissors
- Flower punch
- Hole punches: $3/16$" and $1/16$"
- Black felt-tip marking pen
- Double-sided tape
- Pink button
- 6" length of twine
- $1\frac{1}{2}$"-wide bright pink sheer ribbon
- $1/4$"-wide white satin ribbon
- Raffia

Hatched Chick Easter Surprise

No need to hunt these Easter eggs. They're out in the open and sending happy Easter wishes to a friend or loved one.

Instructions

1. Fold a $10\frac{1}{4}\times7$" card stock rectangle widthwise, with the back extending slightly beyond the front. Trim the back with the decorative-edge scissors. From yellow dotted paper, cut a rectangle slightly smaller than the card front. Trim a short edge of the paper with the cloud decorative-edge scissors 1" less than the card front. Align the lower edges and attach the paper to the card with double-sided tape.

2. Punch two holes in the egg die cut with the $3/16$" hole punch. Pull through raffia and tie it. Punch two holes under the chick's

chin on the other die cut. Pull through white satin ribbon and tie it. Adhere the die cuts to the yellow paper.

3. Punch a flower from blue dotted paper. Adhere the flower to the card. Mark the button holes and punch holes in the card with the $1/16$" hole punch. Pull twine through the holes in the card, blue flower, and button; then tie it into a square knot to secure the button and flower. Write a greeting with the black marking pen across the bottom of the card.

4. Punch two small holes at the top center of the card. Pull through pink ribbon, tie into a bow, and trim the ribbon ends.

—*Designed by Polly McMillan*

Easter with My Three Girls

As vibrant as the Easter eggs themselves, this page bursts with smiling faces, festive color, and cheerful patterns.

Instructions

1. Use decorative-edge scissors to trim the photo. Mount the photo on blue card stock with adhesive. Trim the turquoise card stock about ¼" beyond the edges of the photo. Mount the turquoise card stock on patterned paper, and trim the patterned paper about ¾" beyond the edges of the turquoise card stock.

2. Position the purple-checked vellum over the basket pattern on *page 89* and trace lightly with a pencil. Cut out the basket on the traced lines. Use the oval cutter to cut five eggs from the card stock and patterned papers. To decorate the eggs, use assorted scissors to cut strips of card stock and paper. Mount the strips on the eggs with

adhesive. Use a black marking pen to outline one of the card stock eggs and to write the Easter message on the egg.

3. Cut a large rectangle from the yellow-and-white stripe paper. Mount it on turquoise card stock with adhesive; then trim the edges about ¼" beyond the yellow-and-white paper.

4. Arrange the large layered rectangle, the layered photo, the basket, and the eggs on an 8½×11" sheet of multicolor dot paper. When you are pleased with the arrangement, adhere the pieces to the multicolor dot paper.

5. Cut narrow strips of green card stock for grass; crumple and glue into the basket. Adhere the layered papers to the scrapbook page.

—Designed by Keri Schneider

Materials

Easter with My Three Girls

- Basket pattern on page 89
- Easter photo
- Acid-free card stock: turquoise, green, and bright yellow
- Archival-quality photo album page
- Kangaroo & Joey items as follows:
  - Pink with multicolor dots paper
  - Yellow-and-white stripe paper
  - Stripes with squiggles paper
  - Pink with yellow stripes paper
  - Purple-checked vellum
- Oval cutter
- Decorative-edge scissors
- Acid-free fine-tip black marking pen
- Acid-free adhesive

rectangle on hot pink card stock with adhesive. Trim the hot pink card stock just beyond the edges of the white to create a narrow border. Mount the hot pink rectangle on black card stock. Trim the black card stock about ¼" beyond the edges of the hot pink. Set aside.

2. Mount each photo on hot pink card stock. Trim the card stock just beyond the edges of the photo. Mount the hot pink card stock on white embossed paper and trim to create a ½"-wide border. Mount the embossed paper on hot pink card stock and trim to create a narrow border. Mount the hot pink card stock on black. Trim the black card stock about ¼" beyond the edges of the hot pink.

3. Use the large hole punch to make circles from black card stock. Randomly adhere the circles to the page. Apply the black-and-white-check border stickers close to the edges of the white photo album page. Add another check border sticker about 1" above the bottom border sticker. Center a pink floral border sticker between the two bottom borders. Position a daisy corner sticker at the inside corners formed by the border stickers.

4. Arrange the rectangle with the lettering and the layered photos on the page. When you are pleased with the arrangement, adhere the "Mother's Day" to the page and use a pencil to very lightly mark the corners of the layered photos. Remove the photos from the page.

5. To make the hinge for the photo doors, cut a 1"-wide strip of white card stock slightly shorter than each photo. Fold the strip in half and firmly crease the fold. Apply adhesive to the front of the folded strip and position it along the left edge on the back of the photo. Apply adhesive to the back of the folded strip and position the photo on the page, using the pencil marks for placement. Use the number stickers to add the year below each photo. When the adhesive has set, open the photo flap and use the black marking pen to journal about each photo within the pencil marks. Carefully erase the pencil marks.

—*Designed by Lauren Gick*

Materials

Mother's Day

- Mom and child photos, past and present
- 12"-square archival-quality white album page
- Acid-free card stock: black, hot pink, and white
- White embossed paper
- Me & My Big Ideas items as follows:
  - Black-and-white-check border stickers
  - Floral corner stickers
  - Pink floral border stickers
  - Pink uppercase and lowercase lettering and numeral stickers
- Large hole punch
- Black marking pen
- Acid-free adhesive

Mother's Day

Celebrate Mother's Day by creating a treasured scrapbook page as a gift for Mom. Gather special photos of you, your mother, or other family members; then add journaled memories and sentiments tucked underneath each photo door.

Instructions

1. Use the alphabet stickers to spell "Mother's Day" on white card stock. Trim the white card stock into a long rectangle around the letters. Mount the white

Mother's Day Bouquet

Gather a bouquet of colorful flowers that will still be blooming long after those in the garden are gone. A die-cut basket, embellished with a ribbon and a fabric flower, holds the arrangement and complements a Mother's Day portrait perfectly.

Instructions

1. Mount the photo on white card stock with adhesive. Trim the white card stock about ¼" beyond the edges of the photo. Use the pink marking pen to draw a border on the white card stock.

2. Use the marking pens to add outlines to some of the die cuts, referring to the photo *below* for ideas. Arrange the layered photo and the die cuts on the decorative paper. When you are pleased with the arrangement, adhere the pieces to the paper. Tie a bow with the ribbon. Glue the bow and the fabric flower at the base of the basket handle.

3. Cut a tag from the remaining white card stock. Use the marking pen to write "Mother's Day" and the year on the tag. Tuck one end of the tag under the flower. Adhere the tag in place. Attach the decorative paper to the album page.

—*Designed by Lindsay Ostrom and Vickie Breslin*

Materials

Mother's Day Bouquet

- Mother's Day photo
- Archival-quality photo album page
- White card stock
- Pink paper with white polka dots paper
- Die cuts: basket, flowers, and leaves
- Assorted marking pens, including fine-tip pink
- Acid-free adhesive
- Embellishments:
  - ¼"-wide pink-and-white ribbon
  - Pink fabric flower

Edged in Eyelet

Place a Mother's Day card on the best-dressed list with a fashionably embellished card. Vellum adds sheer appeal.

Instructions

1. Cut 10×7" rectangles from parchment and vellum. Holding the papers together, scallop one narrow end with the decorative-edge scissors. Trim ⅛" from the opposite edge. Align the straight edges; fold the card in half.

2. Referring to the photo *left*, align the scallop edges, and punch teardrops and circles through both layers.

3. Adhere stickers and write messages on the vellum. Center and punch two holes 1½" apart along the fold. Thread ribbon on a needle. From the inside of the card, insert the needle out through each hole and back in, leaving a small loop in each hole on the outside of the card. Thread another piece of ribbon through the loops, leaving a 3" tail at each end. Trim the ribbon ends into a **V**. Tighten the ribbon ends inside the card.

—Designed by Jean Wilson

Materials

Edged in Eyelet
- Pink parchment paper
- White vellum
- Simple Dreams Artist's Collection stickers
- Hole punches: ¹⁄₁₆" and ⅛"
- Teardrop hole punch
- Wide scallop decorative-edge scissors
- Fine-tip black marking pen
- Large-eye tapestry needle
- 18" of 1½"-wide white satin ribbon

For You, Mom
- Card stock: purple, light pink, and white
- Parchment paper: pink, lavender, and beige
- White vellum
- Simple Dreams Artist's Collection stickers
- Black marking pen
- Double-sided foam-adhesive dots
- Green florist's wire

For You, Mom

Here's a twist on stickers. Rather than apply them on the card, back them with vellum and add wire stems to make creative, colorful flowers.

Instructions

1. To make the card, fold a 4¼×8½" light pink card stock rectangle in half widthwise. Print "For You Mom" to fit on 1½×1¾" of white card stock; cut out and layer on varying border widths of pink, lavender, and beige parchment paper. Apply stickers on the Os. Adhere the square to the card, extending beyond the fold.

2. Sandwich wire between stickers and vellum; trim around the petals. From pink card stock cut a flowerpot to the desired size, assemble, and adhere the stems inside the pot. Attach the pot to the card with double-sided foam-adhesive dots.

—Designed by Jean Wilson

Happy Father's Day Accordion

This compact card starts mild-mannered enough. Opened, it shouts a happy message. Change the word or colors to adapt for other occasions.

Instructions

1. Cut a 2×15¾" black paper band. Fold the band widthwise, and accordion-fold it into six sections.

2. Trace the patterns on *page 91* and cut them out. Trace and cut out the letters and the large square onto botanical paper and the smaller rectangle onto black paper.

3. Adhere the pieces to the black band as shown *above*. Write a message with marking pens.

—Designed by Jean Wilson

Top Pop

Double the fun with double Os. Taking their turns as frames, they form a striking design centered in a pair of rhyming words.

Instructions

1. Fold a 7×10" blue paper rectangle widthwise. Line it with slightly smaller white paper.

2. Keeping the text within ½×2", print a message in blue on white paper. Shadow the letters with black. Trace and cut the banner and letter patterns on *page 91*. Trace the banner pattern over the text and cut it out. Adhere the banner to red paper, leaving a narrow margin. Then cut out the banner.

3. Trace and cut out "Top Pop" from red paper. Trim and center the photos in the Os. Adhere the remaining elements.

—Designed by Jean Wilson

Materials

Happy Father's Day Accordion
- Patterns on *page 91*
- Black paper
- Botanical pattern paper
- Tracing paper
- Silver fine-point marking pen
- Black medium-point marking pen
- Liquid adhesive

Top Pop
- Patterns on *page 91*
- Two 1½×1¾" photos
- White paper
- Papers: blue and red polka dot and white
- Tracing paper
- Blue marking pen
- Liquid adhesive

Materials

Father's Day Envelope
- Pattern on *pages 94–95*
- Tracing paper
- 4×6" Father's Day photo
- 12"-square archival-quality photo album page
- Hot Off the Press Paper Pizzazz items as follows:
  - Flowers & Cats paper from the Vintage Papers booklet
  - Pink, cream, and yellow papers from the Plain Pastels booklet
  - Butterfly Punch-Outs from the Watercolor Punch-Outs booklet
- Acid-free black marking pen
- Mini scallop decorative-edge scissors
- Acid-free adhesive

Father's Day Envelope

This envelope-making technique is perfect for Father's Day or Mother's Day pages, and can be adapted for other occasions as well. Try one for Valentine's Day, a birthday, Christmas, a vacation, or a wedding.

Instructions

1. Trace the envelope pattern on *pages 94–95* on tracing paper, making a mirror image of the envelope. Cut out the pattern pieces; then trace on cream paper and cut out.

2. Fold up the envelope bottom as indicated on the pattern piece. Mount the rest of the envelope (with the bottom flap folded) to pink paper. Trim close to the edges.

3. Mount the photograph on yellow paper and trim, leaving a 1/16" border. Open the envelope; and adhere the mounted photo to the envelope. Add journaling to the bottom envelope flap and "Father's Day" on the top flap using the marking pen. Adhere the envelope to the decorative paper, then to the photo album page.

4. Place a butterfly punch-out on the top flap; and use the marking pen to mark a line of dashes near the butterfly and in the lower left corner.

—*Designed by Shauna Berglund-Immel*

To Dad with Love

Handmade lace, angelic cherubs, and a banner put the polish on this homage to Father's Day. It's fun and easy to make your own paper lace with scallop-edge scissors, a hole punch, and rows of marker-drawn dots.

Instructions

1. Use spray adhesive to adhere the hearts and flowers paper to the album page. From the red paper, cut out a large heart and adhere it to the background paper. Glue the red lace trim around the heart.

2. Mount the photo on white paper and trim just beyond the edges of the photo. Mount the white paper on blue paper, and trim to create a ¼"-wide border. Mount the blue paper on white paper and trim to create a ¼"-wide border.

3. Trim the white paper with the decorative-edge scallop scissors. Punch each scallop with the ¹⁄₁₆" hole punch to make the lace edging. Make white dots around the blue border using the white gel pen. Adhere the photo with the layered papers to the red heart.

4. Cut the banner using the die cut. Cut out the center portion and mount the ends and center on solid yellow paper. Trim closely. Use the blue gel pen to write on the banner; then assemble the center and ends with double-sided tape. Adhere to the background page.

5. Cut cherubs out of a second sheet of the same background paper and attach with double-sided foam-adhesive dots to overlap the photo and banner.

—Designed by Shauna Berglund-Immel

Materials

To Dad with Love

- Father's Day photo
- 12"-square archival-quality photo album page
- Banner die cut
- Hearts and Flowers paper
- Papers: blue, pink, red, yellow, and white
- Red lace fabric trim
- Scallop decorative-edge scissors
- White and blue gel pens
- ¹⁄₁₆" hole punch
- Spray adhesive
- Double-sided tape
- Double-sided foam-adhesive dots

fallwinter
celebrations

Magical Halloween

Hocus-pocus! Give your ordinary scrapbook page title a magical makeover using creative lettering. A bubbling cauldron adds an unusual touch as the "O" in Halloween.

Instructions

1. Mount the photo on purple paper with adhesive. Trim the purple paper about ¼" beyond the edges of the photo. Mount the purple paper on black paper. Use the decorative-edge scissors to trim the black paper about ¼" beyond the edges of the purple paper.

2. Refer to *pages 18–19* for instructions on making the Halloween letters. Use a pencil to write lightly "Halloween" on a sheet of white paper. Go over the pencil lines with the black marker and then color in the letters with the brush-tip pens. Trim the white paper into a rectangle around the lettering. Mount the white rectangle on black paper. Trim the black paper about ¼" beyond the edges of the white rectangle. Mount the black rectangle on purple paper and trim the purple paper a scant ¼" beyond the edges of the black paper.

Refer to pages 18–19 ... *pages 18–19* ... *pages 18–19*

3. Trim the green sheet of paper to measure 8×10½". Mount the trimmed green sheet centered on a sheet of black paper. Arrange the layered pieces and Hilda Halloween die-cut pieces on the green sheet. When you are pleased with the arrangement, adhere the pieces to the paper. Use the black fine-tip marker to add the names and date.

—Designed by Jennie Dayley

*C*ast an enchanting spell on your scrapbook pages with creative lettering that spells out your favorite Halloween greeting.

Materials

Magical Halloween
- Halloween photo
- Papers: black, lime green, white, and purple
- EK Success Paperkin Hilda Halloween die-cut set
- Brush- and fine-tip markers: black, orange, and light green
- Decorative-edge scissors
- Liquid adhesive

Trick-or-Treat Bag
- Small white gift bag
- Brush- and fine-tip markers: black and orange

Trick-or-Treat Bag

Need a quick Halloween party favor? Decorate a small white gift bag with Halloween greetings and a checked border. Then fill it with popcorn or candy for each guest.

Instructions

1. Using a pencil, center and lightly draw a 3½×3¾" rectangle onto the front of the bag. Lightly draw three parallel baselines for positioning the words slightly below the center of the square.

2. Complete the lettering as shown on *pages 18–19*. Use the black and orange markers to make the checked border around the lettering. Erase the pencil lines.

—Designed by Jennie Dayley

Materials

Happy Halloween Photo Frame
- Maple Lane Press Ready-to-Make Frame
- Stickopotamus Trick-or-Treat stickers
- Brush- and fine-tip markers: yellow, orange, and black

Witch You Had Been There!
- Halloween photo
- 8½×11" archival-quality photo album page
- 8½×11" paper: orange and white
- Kangaroo & Joey items as follows:
  - Green-and-white-stripe paper (S7)
  - Pumpkin die cut (PDC9)
  - Witch die cut (139DC)
  - Pumpkins die cut (140DC)
  - Black with white dots imprintable paper (109B)
  - Gold-and-white-checked stickers (ST1001)
- Brush- and fine-tip markers: black and yellow
- Acid-free adhesive
- Double-sided foam-adhesive dots

Happy Halloween Photo Frame

As bright and colorful as a piece of candy corn, this picture frame comes alive with Halloween cheer. Liven up the canvas surface of the frame with whimsical lettering and candy corn stickers.

Instructions

1. Color the frame with the yellow marker; allow to dry. Outline the outer and inner edge of the frame with black.

2. To make the lettering, center and lightly draw a pencil baseline at the top and bottom of the frame (be sure to allow enough room to center the height of the letters). The baselines will be your guide for letter placement.

3. Refer to *pages 18–19* for instructions on making the lettering shown on the frame. Use an orange marker to fill in the letters. Erase the pencil lines and outline the letters with the black fine-tip marker.

4. Draw a dashed line around the outer edge of the frame and add details as shown. Adhere candy corn stickers along the sides of the frame.

—Designed by Jennie Dayley

Witch You Had Been There!

Have a bewitching good time composing this collage of colored papers to make a bright Halloween page.

Instructions

1. Trim the striped paper to measure 6½×10". With the bottom edges even, mount the trimmed sheet on the orange paper with adhesive. Apply the border stickers along the side and top edges of the striped paper and about 1" from the bottom edge. Use the black marker to write "Boo!" on the orange paper along the edges of the border stickers and to draw a narrow checked border about ¼" from the orange paper edge.

2. Mount the photo on white paper. Trim the white paper about ½" beyond the edges of the photo. Use the yellow marker to draw a wide border on the white paper. Mount the white paper on the black with white dots paper. Trim the patterned paper about 1" beyond the edges of the white paper.

3. Arrange the layered photo and the die cuts on the page. When you are pleased with the arrangement, adhere the photo using adhesive and the die cuts with double-sided foam-adhesive dots. Use the black marker to write additional messages.

—Designed by Keri Schneider

Holiday Party Invitation

Send out this glitzy party invitation encased in a clear vinyl envelope and set the stage for a dazzling evening of fun.

Instructions

1. From vellum paper, cut the invitation to the desired size.

2. Handwrite or use a computer to print the time, place, and any other information regarding the party.

3. Cut two pieces of vinyl slightly larger than the invitation. With the vinyl pieces together, glue or machine-stitch along three edges to form an envelope.

4. Insert the invitation into the envelope along with the embellishments. Close and secure the open side of the pocket as in *Step 3*.

5. Use decorative-edge scissors to trim the invitation.

—Designed by Vicki Breslin

Materials

Holiday Party Invitation
- Vellum paper
- Embellishments: confetti, glitter, and curly ribbon
- Clear vinyl
- Decorative-edge scissors
- Plastic glue, waterbed glue, or a sewing machine
- Computer and printer (optional)

2. To cover the outside of the booklet, cut a piece of decorative paper 1" wider and longer than each piece of cardboard. Spray adhesive on one side of each piece of cardboard. With the adhesive side facing down, center and adhere the cardboard to the wrong side of the decorative paper. Carefully smooth the paper with your fingers. Attach strips of double-sided tape along each inside edge of the cardboard, and wrap the decorative paper over the edges toward the inside, adhering it to the tape. Miter the corners of the paper for a smooth fit.

3. Lay the two pieces of cardboard covers side-by-side, and measure the total outer dimensions. Cut a piece of card stock slightly smaller than the total measurement of the covers. **Note:** *The card stock should hide the raw edges of the decorative paper on the inside of the cover.* Fold the card stock in half. Spray adhesive on the inside of the cardboard pieces and adhere the covers to the outside of the folded card stock. Embellish as desired.

Dimensional Embossed Christmas Card

Create ornate dimensional designs on booklet-style Christmas cards using rubber stamps on solidly embossed pieces of paper. Make various shapes of dimensional embossed papers using this technique. Then combine with elegant papers to create one-of-a-kind greeting cards.

Instructions

1. Decide on the booklet dimensions and cut two pieces of lightweight cardboard or mat board to the desired size. Following the instructions for the booklet-style cards, cover the outside with decorative paper such as the gold crinkle paper shown on two of the cards *above*, or use the paper of your choice. Finish the inside if desired.

Materials

Booklet-Style Christmas Card
- Lightweight cardboard or mat board
- Card stock in desired colors
- Variety of decorative papers: mulberry, suede, crinkled, or handmade
- Spray adhesive
- Double-sided tape

Booklet-Style Christmas Card

When a simple card is not enough to celebrate the occasion, make an elegant booklet using lightweight cardboard or mat board. Decorate with dimensional embossing and luxurious embellishments of braids, tassels, ribbons, or beads. Adorn the inside with exquisite papers to coordinate with the cover.

Instructions

1. Decide on the booklet dimensions and cut two pieces of lightweight cardboard or mat board to the desired size.

2. From card stock, cut a shape like that of the stamp being used. (See the shapes of the card stock with stamp embossing on the cards *opposite.*) Ink the entire surface of the card stock with gold embossing ink by rubbing it across an ink pad.

3. While the ink is still wet, sprinkle gold or another color of embossing powder over the entire inked surface (see *Step 1*).

4. Heat the embossing powder with a heat-embossing tool until it melts and becomes glossy (see *Step 2*); let it cool.

5. Repeat the process of sprinkling and heating the embossing powder to create layers (two or three times are usually enough).

6. Working quickly before the last layer of embossing powder cools, ink the stamp in merlot ink, and press it into the soft layers of embossing powder. Pull the stamp up quickly, leaving an inked impression (see *Step 3*).

7. Tear a piece of mulberry paper slightly larger than the stamp-embossed design. For easier tearing, moisten the paper fibers along the tear line with a paintbrush dampened with water. Mount the stamp-embossed paper on the mulberry paper.

8. Adhere the layered stamp-embossed papers to the booklet and embellish as desired. **Note:** *For a more dramatic effect, edge some of the paper layers with strips of contrasting paper or with tiny glass beads without holes that frame the design as shown on the holly card,* opposite.

9. Use the gold marking pen to write a holiday greeting.

—*Designed by Suzanne State*

Step 1

Step 2

Step 3

Create stamped decorative paper to coordinate with your stamp-embossed greeting card, as shown above.

Materials
Dimensional Embossed Christmas Card
- Lightweight cardboard or matboard
- Card stock in desired colors
- Mulberry paper
- Posh Impressions stamps: Christmas Cone (Z375E), Jingling Bells (Z841F), Ribbon Bells (Z806H), and Holly Sprig (Z153C)
- Embossing ink pads: gold and merlot red
- Embossing powder
- Heat-embossing tool
- Gold marking pen
- Small paintbrush
- Double-sided tape
- Embellishments: braid, tassels, ribbon, beads, or narrow strips of metallic tape

Materials

Elegant Party Invitation

- White card stock
- Swirl design paper
- Moet & Chandon rubber stamp
- Gold embossing ink pad
- Gold embossing powder
- Heat-embossing tool
- Seal and wax
- Gold marking pen
- Liquid adhesive
- Spray adhesive
- Soft paintbrush
- 1" -wide blue sheer ribbon

Elegant Party Invitation

Combine embossed stamping, elegant paper, and a wax seal to create easy party invitations that look as if you spent a fortune to have them made.

Instructions

1. Determine the desired size of the invitation. Cut out, fold in half, and crease the card stock to create the invitation.

2. Cut the swirl paper to fit the front of the card. Use spray adhesive to adhere the swirl paper to the front of the card.

3. To make the stamp-embossed rectangle on the front, press the rubber stamp onto the gold embossing ink pad, then onto the white card stock. While the ink is wet, quickly sprinkle gold embossing powder over the stamped image.

4. Shake off the excess powder and use a soft paintbrush to sweep loose powder

from around the design, if necessary. Return excess powder to the container.

5. Use the heat-embossing tool to melt the powder until it becomes glossy, forming the embossed design.

6. Lay the blue sheer ribbon on the card and adhere the embossed card on top of the ribbon.

7. To make an imprint, light the wick on the stick of sealing wax and let it drip onto the corner of the embossed card (see example, *Step 1, opposite*). Before the wax cools, press the seal onto a gold ink pad, then into the soft wax (see example, *Step 2, opposite*). The ink helps the seal to release, and the imprint will remain in the wax.

8. Complete the invitation by using the gold marking pen to write the party information inside, including the time and place.

Peace, Love, Joy

There's a definite difference between cards you make and cards you buy—recipients will notice and cherish your personal touch and message.

Instructions

1. Determine the desired size of the greeting card. Cut out, fold in half, and crease the white card stock to create the card.

2. Cut the terra-cotta paper to fit the front of the card. Using spray adhesive, adhere the paper to the front of the card.

3. Cut graduated sizes of the swirl, gold, and off-white papers allowing enough space around each piece to create the appearance of a "frame" when the papers are layered.

4. To make the stamp-embossed rectangle on the front, press the rubber stamp onto the gold embossing ink pad, then onto the off-white card stock rectangle.

5. While the ink is wet, sprinkle gold embossing powder over the stamped image.

6. Shake off the excess powder. Use a soft paintbrush to sweep loose powder from around the design. Return excess powder to the container.

7. Use the heat-embossing tool to melt the powder until it becomes glossy, forming the embossed design.

8. Mount the off-white embossed paper on the gold paper with adhesive. Trim the gold paper just beyond the edges of the white to create a ¼" narrow border. Mount the gold on the swirl paper. Trim the swirl

paper to create a border of ½" to ¾". Center and adhere the layers to the front of the card.

9. Glue a piece of braid to the card near the fold.

—Designed by Suzanne State

Step 1

Step 2

Materials

Peace, Love, Joy

- Card stock: white and off-white
- Swirl design paper
- Paper: gold and terra-cotta
- Peace, love, and joy rubber stamp
- Gold embossing ink pad
- Gold embossing powder
- Heat-embossing tool
- Spray adhesive
- Liquid adhesive
- Soft paintbrush
- Braid embellishment

Stamp bags with stars of different sizes and in various colors. To close the bags, use a star-shape hole punch to make holes for ribbon or a gilded twig. Or use sealing wax and a seal to secure the bag.

To decorate a papier-mâché box, paint it white and stamp it with gold metallic acrylic paint.

Materials
Embossed Gift Bags
- White paper sacks, various sizes
- Rubber stamps
- Clear embossing ink pad
- Metallic embossing powders: silver, gold, and blue
- Heat-embossing tool
- Soft paintbrush
- Optional embellishments: sheer and satin ribbon, gold cord, buttons, star hole punch, and gift cards

Embossed Gift Bags

Rubber stamps and embossing powder transform ordinary paper bags into elegant gift packages.

Instructions

1. Ink the rubber stamp and press onto a paper sack.

2. While the ink is wet, quickly sprinkle embossing powder in the desired color over the stamped image.

3. Shake off the excess powder; use a soft paintbrush to remove loose powder around the design if necessary. Return loose powder to the container.

4. Use the heat-embossing tool to melt the powder until it becomes glossy, forming the embossed design. Repeat for multiple embossed images.

5. To keep the sack closed, fold the top of the sack and punch holes with the star punch. Weave gold cord or ribbon through the holes.

Hanukkah Traditions

Add a personal touch to Hanukkah this year by sending handmade cards you've made for the celebration.

Instructions

1. Use spray adhesive to adhere the snowflake paper to the front of the card, trimming the edges even with the card.

2. Cut a 2" square in the upper center of the card front. Remove the square and place the square cutout on silver paper. Trace around the square with a pencil, and trim the edges as though you were matting the traced square. Place the silver square on navy paper; adhere the edges and trim as before.

3. Cut out the center of the 2" silver square through the silver and navy layers to make a silver frame matted on navy paper. Place the frame over the window on the card front and glue it in place.

4. Cover the inside back of the card with silver paper; then center a 4½×6" light blue rectangle over the silver paper. Glue it in place. Using the pattern on *page 89*, cut the menorah out of silver paper. Cut nine candle tapers out of navy paper and punch nine teardrops for the flames out of gold paper. Position the pieces in the center of the light blue rectangle and glue the pieces in place.

5. Cover the inside front of the card with white vellum and trim the edges even with the card. Write "Happy Hanukkah" below the menorah with the silver marking pen.

—*Designed by Susan Cobb*

Materials

Hanukkah Traditions

- Menorah and candle patterns on *page 89*
- Blank white 5×6½" card
- Paper: light blue and navy
- White vellum
- Hot Off the Press Paper Pizzazz items as follows:
  - Snowflake paper from the Christmas booklet
  - Silver metallic paper from the Pearlescent Papers booklet
  - Gold metallic paper from the Metallics booklet
- Silver marking pen
- Teardrop hole punch
- Liquid adhesive
- Spray adhesive

Display the menorah in a framed window created from vellum.

Gold and Silver Leafing

Tip: *For flat background areas, such as the gold on the Christmas ornaments,* right, *brush leafing adhesive onto the paper, and let it sit for 15 minutes. Lay the leafing material on the adhesive and gently smooth with a tissue or soft paintbrush. Apply the hotmelt adhesive details on top of the first layer of leafing material.*

Materials

Gilded Card and Gift Tag

- Blank 5×7" greeting card or card stock to make your own card
- Sheets of gold, silver, copper, or patterned leafing material
- Leafing adhesive
- Transfer paper
- Glue gun and hotmelt adhesive
- Soft paintbrush and old toothbrush
- Fine-tip glue pen

Gilded Card and Gift Tag

Draw your own holiday images or refer to the examples *above and opposite* for card or gift tag ideas.

Step 1

Step 2

Step 3

Instructions

1. Cut out, fold in half, and crease the card stock to create cards the size you want. Using a glue gun, draw your own design onto the front of the card (see *Step 1*). Let the adhesive lines dry until they have hardened but are still tacky.

2. Place a sheet of leafing material over the hardened design, and press it onto the adhesive with your finger (see *Step 2*).

3. Using an old toothbrush, brush the excess leafing material away from the design (see *Step 3*). **Note:** *To fill in background areas with leafing material, see the Gold and Silver Leafing Tip, top left.*

4. Cut a 2¼×3¾" gift tag from card stock. Use the paintbrush to apply the leafing adhesive to make a border around the tag; let the adhesive dry according to the manufacturer's instructions. Repeat *Steps 2 and 3, left.*

5. Using the glue pen, write a name or greeting in the center of the gift tag; then press the leafing material to the glue. Remove excess as instructed earlier.

—*Designed by Becky Lau Ekstrand*

As our marriage brings
new meaning to love
so our love
brings new meaning
to life.

wedding day
wishes

Arlene & Nelson
request the pleasure
of your company
at their marriage
Saturday,
the first of October
nineteen hundred and ninety-four
Kahala Hilton
Honolulu, Hawaii

Sometimes a little help is the best gift for a busy bride. Offer your creativity for accessories such as invitations, elegant gift boxes, and decorations for the reception. After the wedding, give the newlyweds a scrapbook of wedding reminders that will last a lifetime.

Materials

Wedding Thank-You
- 5½×8½" piece of white card stock
- Handmade petal paper (available at art supply stores)
- "Thank You" rubber stamp
- Gold pigment ink
- Gold embossing powder
- Spray adhesive
- Xyron machine and adhesive (optional)
- Heat-embossing tool
- Creasing tool (bone folder)
- Envelope

Wedding Gift Box
- Flat stampable box or ready-made box
- Handmade petal paper (available at art supply stores)
- Spray adhesive
- Xyron machine and adhesive (optional)
- 29" length of ½"-wide sheer ribbon

Wedding Thank-You

For a thank-you note as personal as the sentiments penned inside, make personalized cards that each wedding guest will cherish.

Instructions

1. To make the note card, cut the handmade paper the same size as the card stock.

2. Spray the handmade paper with spray adhesive. Press the handmade paper to the white card stock; then fold in half using a creasing tool for a clean fold. **Note:** *If you are using a Xyron machine, run the handmade paper through the machine to apply adhesive.*

3. Stamp the card with the gold ink, sprinkle embossing powder on the ink, and finish with a heat-embossing tool.

Wedding Gift Box

A box made of delicate rose petal paper holds a small gift for each wedding party participant.

Instructions

1. Cut the handmade paper to fit the box and spray it with spray adhesive. Press it onto the sides of the box. **Note:** *If you are using a Xyron machine, run the handmade paper through the machine to apply adhesive.*

2. Fold the flat box along the prescored lines and assemble to make a dimensional box.

3. Fill the box as desired and embellish with ribbon.

—*Designed by Marjorie Huber*

Turn a simple paper tent into a birdseed container.

Materials

For All Containers
- Gold pigment ink
- Gold embossing powder
- Heat-embossing tool

Rose Gift Box
- White precut square box
- 1¼×2½" rectangle of white card stock
- Rubber stamps: rose and thank you
- Gold marking pen
- ⅛" hole punch
- Silk flowers
- Gold cord
- 1½"-wide sheer ribbon

Wedding Accessories

Send wedding guests home with a memento of the special day. Fold a doily around a message of thanks, give a container of birdseed, or offer tiny decorated boxes to hold cake or candies from the reception.

Instructions

To emboss, stamp the selected images on the paper or ribbon with pigment ink. Immediately sprinkle with gold embossing powder. Tilt the paper or ribbon up on edge and tap off the excess powder. Hold the paper or ribbon near a heat-embossing tool until the powder melts, creating a shiny, raised image.

Rose Gift Box
1. Emboss roses on the unassembled box. Assemble the box.

2. For the gift tag, fold the card stock rectangle in half. Emboss a single rose on the front of the gift tag and "Thank You" inside.

3. Tie the ribbon in a bow around the box. Thread gold cord through a hole punched in the top corner of the tag; knot the cord around the center of the ribbon bow. Slip silk flowers inside the ribbon knot.

Love and Marriage Envelope
1. From the decorative paper, cut a 9¼" square; using double-sided tape adhere the decorative paper centered on the wrong side of the doily.

2. Cut the typing paper to the size of the envelope and handwrite the message with the gold marking pen. Place the message inside the envelope.

3. Turn the decorative paper and doily so a corner is at the top; tape the envelope centered on the decorative paper.

4. Fold in the corners of the doily over the envelope in this order: sides, bottom, and top.

5. Emboss the doves on the grosgrain ribbon. From the white card stock, cut a heart and emboss "Love and Marriage" and a rose on the white heart. Center and tape the heart to the embossed grosgrain ribbon. Layer sheer ribbon on top. Wrap the layered ribbons around the envelope; secure the ends at the back with a Velcro circle.

Birdseed Packet

1. Score and crease the large piece of decorative card stock 3", 6", and 7" from one short edge; fold on the score lines, creating a tent shape with a ½"-wide end tab. Tape the ribbon on the tent ¼" from the right edge.

2. Tape a small bag of birdseed inside the tent. Place double-sided tape on the outside of the end tab; press the opposite edge of the tent bottom onto the tape.

3. Emboss the marriage saying on the 2⅜×1¾" rectangle of white card stock. Use double-sided tape to layer the saying on the gold card stock and then on the packet front. Use hotmelt adhesive to glue a flower and bow below the message.

Embossed Birds Box

1. Emboss "Love and Marriage" and roses on the lid of the unassembled box and doves on the sides. Assemble the box. Use hotmelt adhesive to glue the leaves and berries to the lid and tie the ribbon into a bow.

—*Designed by Suzanne State*

Materials

Love and Marriage Envelope
- 1 sheet each of decorative paper, white card stock, and white typing paper
- 10" square paper doily
- Vellum envelope (note card size)
- 2" white paper heart
- Rubber stamps: rose, love and marriage, and three doves
- Double-sided tape
- Velcro self-adhesive circle
- 1⅜"-wide white grosgrain ribbon
- 1½"-wide sheer ribbon

Birdseed Packet
- 3×7½" decorative white card stock
- 2⅜×1¾" decorative white card stock
- 2⅝×2" gold card stock
- Rubber stamp with marriage quote
- Double-sided tape
- Glue gun and hotmelt adhesive
- Creasing tool (bone folder)
- 7½" length of 1⅜"-wide ribbon
- Small clear resealable bag
- Birdseed
- Silk flowers

Embossed Birds Box
- Precut rectangle box
- Stamps: rose, love and marriage, and three doves
- 1½"-wide sheer ribbon
- Silk leaves and berries
- Glue gun and hotmelt adhesive

Wedding Moments

Make an elegant interactive scrapbook page that need not be removed from the protective sleeve each time you look at it. Simply cut a window in the protector to allow the center card to be untied and read.

Instructions

1. Crop and mount photos on decorative paper using the adhesive. Adhere the mounted photos at the corners of the scrapbook page. Adhere decorative paper to the scrapbook page with spray adhesive.

2. Referring to the diagram on *page 90*, cut a piece from the 12"-square card stock and from the coordinating paper. Fold the card stock and paper following the fold lines shown on the diagram. Unfold the card and paper, and cut the outer flaps into triangle points. Trim the paper slightly smaller than the outside card stock and adhere the coordinating paper to the inside of the card with spray adhesive.

3. Cut a 3" square of vellum, write and print the message, and place it in the inside center of the card. Referring to the diagram, punch two holes at the top of the vellum square going through the card. Fold a 6"-length of ribbon in half and thread the ends through the holes from front to back. Thread the ends from the back through the opposite holes as shown in the photo, *above left*, and trim the ribbon ends as desired. Fold in the card flaps; then center and punch a hole along each of the inner folds as shown in the diagram. Center and cut a ¼"-long slit along each of the outer folds as shown.

4. Weave the 18" length of ribbon through one of the slits from front to back. Continue weaving the ribbon through the holes, around the back of the card, through the opposite pair of holes, and back through the opposite slit. Close the card by tying the ribbon ends. Adhere the card to the center of the scrapbook page. Place stickers where desired.

—Designed by Arlene Santos

Materials

Wedding Moments
- Diagram on *page 90*
- Wedding photos
- 12"-square white scrapbook page
- 12"-square patterned papers
- 12"-square piece of light pink card stock or desired color
- Iridescent polka-dot vellum paper
- Wedding or floral stickers
- Acid-free adhesive
- Acid-free spray adhesive
- Paper punch with small holes
- 6" and 18" lengths of ⅜"-wide coordinating ribbon
- Computer and printer (optional)

Punched Paper Lace

Add a touch of refined elegance with delicate paper doilies and fans for additional decorations at the reception.

Instructions

Trace the desired pattern from *page 94* onto a piece of typing paper. Cut out the pattern, including the shaded portions, using the decorative and hole punches. Set the patterns aside.

Punched Lace Doily

1. Referring to the folding diagram on *page 94*, fold the rice paper in quarters; open up the last fold (the square will be folded in half), then fold the half-square into eighths. Trace the pattern onto one side of the folded paper shape.

2. Align and punch the shaded areas first; then trim off the outer points. For best results, punch through two or three folds/layers of paper at a time, retracing the pattern as necessary to complete the designs.

3. Following the pattern, sew the round crystal beads and the seed beads to the doily using a single strand of white thread. Sew a round crystal bead and an elongated bicone crystal bead to each point of the octagon doily.

Punched Lace Fan

1. Carefully mark dots at 1⅝" intervals along the long edges of the 4½×14" rice paper strip. Fold the strip in accordion pleats, matching the dots.

2. Trace the pattern on *page 94* onto one side of the folded paper shape. For best results, punch through only two or three folds/layers of the paper at a time, retracing the pattern as necessary to complete the design. Punch out the shaded portions first; then cut along the outlines to make scallops.

3. Following the pattern, sew the seed and bugle beads to the fan using a single strand of white thread. Thread silk ribbon through the punched holes along the bottom edge of the fan; tie a bow.

Punched Lace Candy Cups

Randomly punch small stars and circles into the sides of the cupcake or candy papers. Trim the cups with decorative-edge scissors.

—*Designed by Laura Collins*

Materials

Punched Lace Doily
- Pattern on *page 94*
- 14" square of thin rice paper
- Decorative paper punches: 1"-wide daisy, ⅝"-wide flower, and 1"-wide four-hearts
- Tracing paper
- Small circle hole punch
- 8 elongated 13×6-mm bicone, small-hole crystal beads
- 32—4-mm round, small-hole crystal beads
- 1 package clear glass seed beads
- White sewing thread
- Beading needle

Punched Lace Fan
- Pattern on *page 94*
- 4½×14" strip of thin rice paper
- 1"-wide daisy paper punch
- Small circle paper punch
- Red glass seed beads
- Green small bugle beads
- Tracing paper
- White sewing thread
- Beading needle
- 2 yards of ¼"-wide white silk ribbon

Punched Lace Candy Cups
- Cupcake and candy cups
- Small star and small circle paper punches
- Decorative-edge scissors

Materials

Pocket Keepsake Page
- Photos and mementos
- White card stock
- Anna Griffin items as follows:
  - Three 12"-square sheets each of Pink & Green Stripes paper (AG014)
  - Pink & Yellow floral paper (AG017)
  - Die-cut Rose (LC401)
- $9/16$"-wide seam binding ribbon
- Double-sided tape
- Frame with 12"-square opening (optional)

Pocket Keepsake Page

Take your inspiration from a scrapbook page. Frame cherished wedding photos and mementos in a filigree frame; then display on a table to enjoy throughout the year.

Instructions

1. From the same decorative paper, cut one $2\times10\frac{3}{4}$" strip, one $5\frac{1}{2}\times10\frac{3}{4}$" strip, and one $9\frac{1}{4}\times10\frac{3}{4}$" rectangle for the pockets.

2. Use double-sided tape to attach seam binding ribbon along the top, left, and right edges on the front of each pocket. Tape the ribbon ends to the underside of the pockets.

3. On the back of the pockets, apply double-sided tape along the bottom, left, and right edges. Position the large pocket on the remaining sheet of floral paper with the top edge of the pocket about $2\frac{1}{2}$" from the top of the sheet. With the bottom and side edges aligned, position the medium pocket on the large pocket, and the small pocket on the medium pocket. Press the pockets together firmly along the taped edges.

4. Tuck photographs and mementos inside the pockets, securing them with double-sided tape if desired. From the card stock, cut a long thin rectangular strip of paper. Personalize the rectangular strip with handwriting or print with a computer. Tape the strip to the small pocket. Attach the rose die cut with double-sided tape. Insert the page into a frame.

—Designed by Anna Griffin

Materials
A Contemporary Announcement
• Mint green card stock
• Clear vellum
• Hero Arts Rubber Stamps background stamp
• Marking pens: blue and purple
• Vargas computer font
• 2 tiny brass fasteners
• Envelopments purple envelope
• 1/8" hole punch
• Computer and printer
• Repositionable adhesive
• 2/3 yard of 1/2"-wide purple silk ribbon

A Contemporary Announcement

A celebration of quiet elegance emanates from this artistic wedding invitation. Topped by hand-stamped clear vellum, the printed invitation is sashed in a cummerbund of paper and royal purple silk ribbon.

Instructions

1. From the mint green card stock, cut the invitation to measure 5×7"; then use a computer printer to print the words on the smooth side of the paper. The invitation information should not cover more than 3½×5¼". From the mint green paper, also cut a 2×10¾" band.

2. Color the stamp with the markers, placing purple in the center and blue at the ends. Stamp the clear vellum, then cut a rectangle to measure 4½×6¼". Fasten the vellum to the mint green card stock in the upper corners with tiny brass fasteners.

3. Wrap the band, textured side out, around the invitation and secure the ends of the band in back with a dot of repositionable adhesive. Tie the purple ribbon around the band. Place the invitation in the center of the envelope and close.

—*Designed by Shannon Smith*

Patterns

Accordion-Fold Birthday Card
page 39

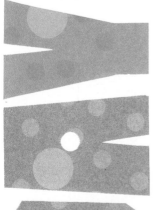

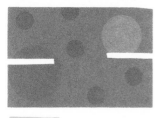

Glue to Opposite Flap

Rocking Horse Shower Invitation
page 25

Fold

Fold and glue to outside of larger flaps

Punch

Fold

NOTE: Make this flap the same size as the opposite flap

M   V   V   M

Fold   Fold   Fold   Fold

5½"

1⅜"   2"   4"   2"   1⅜"

10¾"

Diagram A

M   M   V   V   M   M

Fold Fold Fold   Fold Fold Fold

4¾"

1⅜" 1⅜" 1¼" 2½" 1¼" 1⅜" 1⅜"

10½"

Diagram B

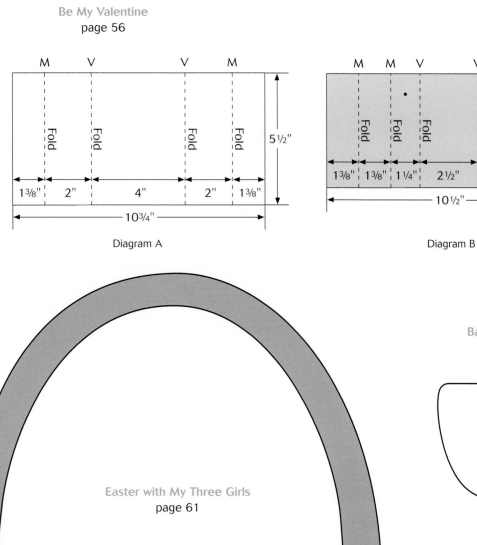

Easter with My Three Girls
page 61

Baby Carriage Announcement
page 26

Baby Buggy
Cut 1

Hanukkah Traditions
page 77

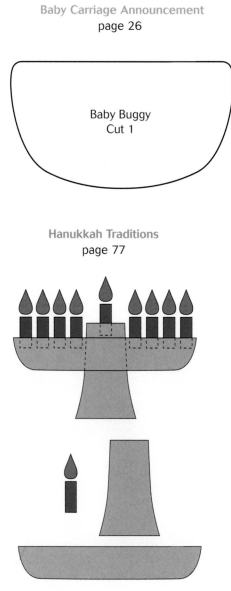

Patterns

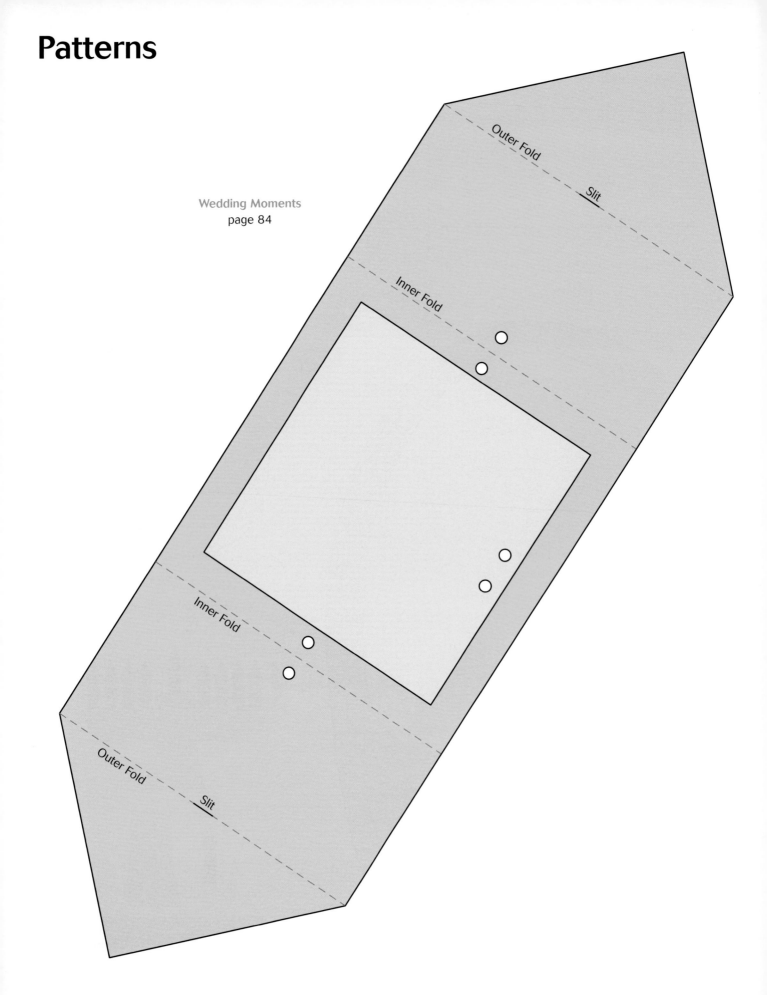

Wedding Moments
page 84

Outer Fold

Slit

Inner Fold

Inner Fold

Outer Fold

Slit

Happy Father's Day
to the

Top Pop
page 65

Happy Father's Day Accordion
page 65

TOP

HAPPY

Father's Day

Love

Patterns

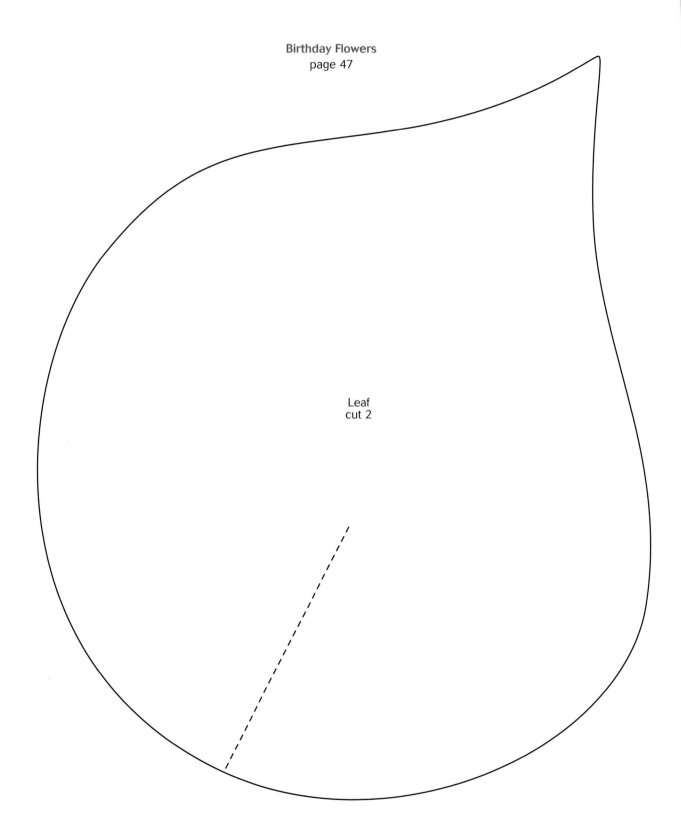

Birthday Flowers
page 47

Leaf
cut 2

Birthday Flowers
page 47

Back Petals

Middle Petals

Place on Fold

Front Petals

Place on Fold

Patterns

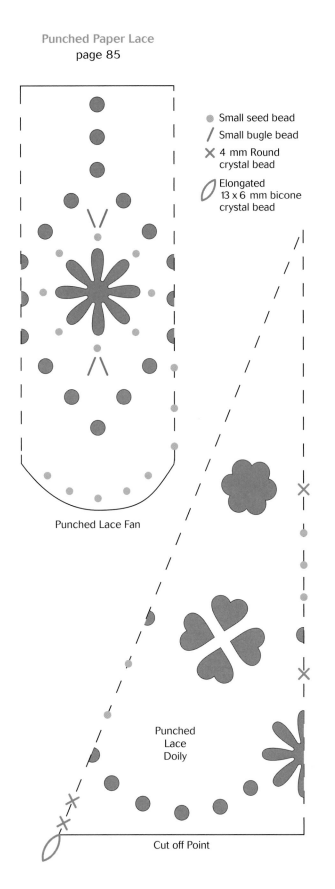

Punched Paper Lace
page 85

- Small seed bead
/ Small bugle bead
✕ 4 mm Round crystal bead
⫰ Elongated 13 x 6 mm bicone crystal bead

Punched Lace Fan

Punched
Lace
Doily

Cut off Point

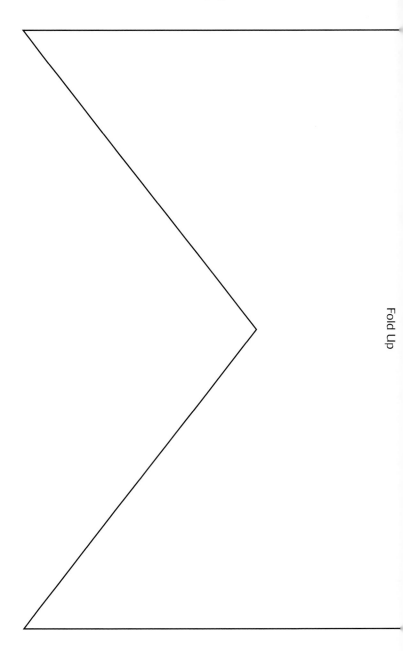

Father's Day Envelope
page 66

Fold Up

Punched Lace Doily
page 85

Folding Diagram

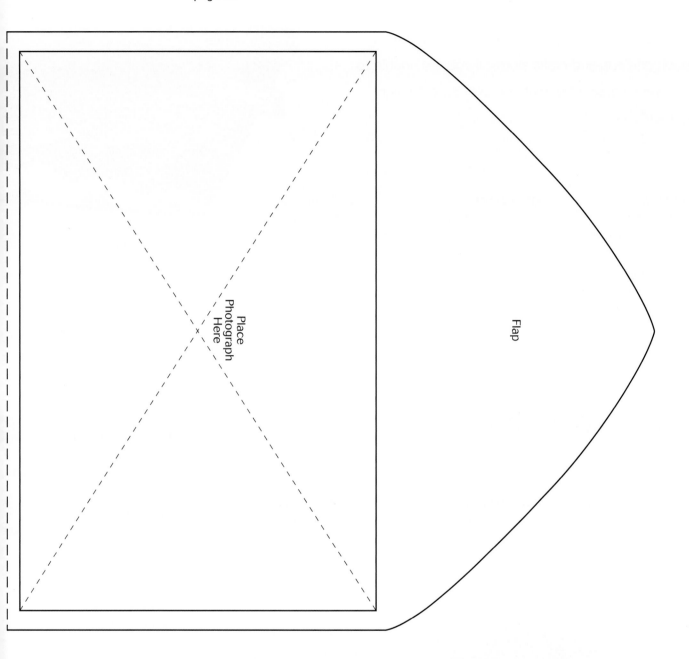

Place
Photograph
Here

Flap

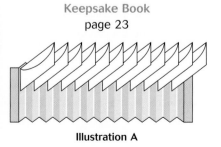

Illustration A

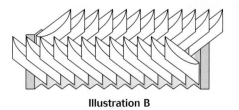

Illustration B

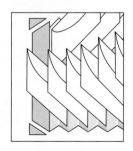

Illustration C

Source List

The sources given for project materials are available at scrapbook and arts-and-crafts stores. If you are unable to locate an item, contact the manufacturer for a retailer located near you.

A

All Night Media
800/STAMPED
www.plaidonline.com
Art Accents
360/733-8989
www.artaccents.net
Art Gone Wild
800/945-3980
(No website address)

B

Beary Patch (The)
877/327-2111
www.bearypatchinc.com

C

Cut-It-Up
916/646-4646
www.scrapramento.com

D

Debbie Mumm
509/466-3572
www.debbiemumm.com

E – G

EK Success
800/524-1349
www.eksuccess.com
Ellison Craft & Design
800/253-2238
(No website address)
Envelopments
714/258-2900
www.envelopments.com
Ever After
800/646-0010
(No website address)
Griffin, Anna Inc.
888/817-8170
www.annagriffin.com

H – J

Hero Arts
800/822-HERO (4376)
www.heroarts.com
Hot Off the Press
503/266-9102
www.hotp.com

K – M

K&Company
888/244-2083
www.kandcompany.com
Kangaroo & Joey
800/646-8065
www.kangarooandjoey.com
Maple Lane Press
(see EK Success)
Me & My Big Ideas
949/589-4607
www.meandmybigideas.com
Mrs. Grossman's
800/429-4549
www.mrsgrossmans.com

N – O

Notations
408/257-5505
www.notations.net/Paper Reflections

P – Q

Paper Flair
(see Hot Off the Press)
Paper Pizzazz
(see Hot Off the Press)
Paper Reflections
(see Notations)
Posh Impressions
800/421-7674
www.poshimpressions.com
Provo Craft
800/937-7686
www.provocraft.com

Printworks Collection
562/906-1262
(No website address)
PSX
800/782-6748
www.psxdesign.com

R

Ranger Industries, Inc.
800/244-2211
www.rangerink.com
Rubber Stampede
800/632-8386
www.rubberstampede.com

S – Z

Sea Shells
(see Ranger Industries, Inc.)
Simple Dreams
(see Stampin' Buddies)
Sonburn, Inc.
925/239-2888
Stampin' Buddies
978/774-5057
www.stampinbuddies.com
Stampin' Up
800/STAMPUP
www.stampinup.com
Stickopotamus
(see EK Success)